SHEPHERD'S NOTES

Shepherd's Notes Titles Available

SHEPHERD'S NOTES COMMENTARY SERIES

Old Testament

0-80549-028-0	Genesis	0-80549-341-7	Psalms 101-150
0-80549-056-6	Exodus	0-80549-016-7	Proverbs
0-80549-069-8	Leviticus & Numbers	0-80549-059-0	Ecclesiastes, Song of
0-80549-027-2	Deuteronomy		Solomon
0-80549-058-2	Joshua & Judges	0-80549-197-X	Isaiah
0-80549-057-4	Ruth & Esther	0-80549-070-1	Jeremiah-
0-80549-063-9	1 & 2 Samuel		Lamentations
0-80549-007-8	1 & 2 Kings	0-80549-078-7	Ezekiel
0-80549-064-7	1 & 2 Chronicles	0-80549-015-9	Daniel
0-80549-194-5	Ezra, Nehemiah	0-80549-326-3	Hosea-Obadiah
0-80549-006-X	Job	0-80549-334-4	Jonah-Zephaniah
0-80549-339-5	Psalms 1-50	0-80549-065-5	Haggai-Malachi
0-80549-340-9	Psalms 51-100		

New Testament

1-55819-688-9	Matthew	1-55819-689-7	Philippians,
0-80549-071-X	Mark		Colossians, &
0-80549-004-3	Luke		Philemon
1-55819-693-5	John	0-80549-000-0	1 & 2 Thessalonians
1-55819-691-9	Acts	1-55819-692-7	1 & 2 Timothy, Titus
0-80549-005-1	Romans	0-80549-336-0	Hebrews
0-80549-325-5	1 Corinthians	0-80549-018-3	James
0-80549-335-2	2 Corinthians	0-80549-019-1	1 & 2 Peter & Jude
1-55819-690-0	Galatians	0-80549-214-3	1, 2 & 3 John
0-80549-327-1	Ephesians	0-80549-017-5	Revelation

SHEPHERD'S NOTES CHRISTIAN CLASSICS

0-80549-347-6	Mere Christianity-	0-80549-394-8	Miracles-C.S.Lewis
	C.S.Lewis	0-80549-196-1	Lectures to My
0-80549-353-0	The Problem of Pain/		Students-Charles
	A Grief Observed-		Haddon Spurgeon
	C.S.Lewis	0-80549-220-8	The Writings of Justin
0-80549-199-6	The Confessions-		Martyr
	Augustine		
0-80549-200-3	Calvin's Institutes	0-80549-345-X	The City of God

SHEPHERD'S NOTES-BIBLE SUMMARY SERIES

0-80549-377-8	Old Testament	0-80549-385-9	Life & Letters of Paul
0-80549-378-6	New Testament	0-80549-376-X	Manners & Customs
0-80549-384-0	Life & Teachings of		of Bible Times
	Jesus	0-80549-380-8	Basic Christian Beliefs

SHEPHERD'S NOTES

When you need a guide through the Scriptures

Galatians

BROADMAN
&HOLMAN
PUBLISHERS

Nashville, Tennessee

Shepherd Notes—*Galatians*

© 1997 Broadman & Holman Publishers, Nashville, Tennessee

All rights reserved

Printed in the United States of America

ISBN# 1–55819–690–0

Dewey Decimal Classification: 227.4

Subject Heading: BIBLE N.T. GALATIANS

Library of Congress Card Catalog Number: 97–25036

Library of Congress Cataloging-in-Publication Data

Galatians / Dana Gould, editor

    p. cm.—(Shepherd's notes)

    Includes bibliographical references.

    ISBN 1–55819–690–0 (tp)

        1. Bible. N.T. Galatians—Study and teaching.

    I. Gould, Dana, 1951–. II. Series.

BS2685.5.G35   1997

227'.407—DC21

                                          97–25036

                                            CIP

4 5 6 7 8 9   06 05 04 03

CONTENTS

FOREWORD

Dear Reader:

Shepherd's Notes are designed to give you a quick, step-by-step overview of every book of the Bible. They are not meant to be a substitute for the biblical text; rather, they are study guides intended to help you explore the wisdom of Scripture in personal or group study and to apply that wisdom successfully in your own life.

Shepherd's Notes guide you through both the main themes of each book of the Bible and illuminate fascinating details through appropriate commentary and reference notes. Historical and cultural background information brings the Bible into sharper focus.

Six different icons, used throughout the series, call your attention to historical-cultural information, Old Testament and New Testament references, word pictures, unit summaries, and personal application for everyday life.

Whether you are a novice or a veteran at Bible study, I believe you will find *Shepherd's Notes* a resource that will take you to a new level in your mining and applying the riches of Scripture.

In Him,

David R. Shepherd
Editor-in-Chief

DESIGNED FOR THE BUSY USER

Shepherd's Notes for Galatians is designed to provide an easy-to-use tool for getting a quick handle on Galatians' important features, and for gaining an understanding of the message of this New Testament epistle. Information available in more difficult-to-use reference works has been incorporated into the *Shepherd's Notes* format. This brings you the benefits of many more advanced and expensive works packed into one small volume.

Shepherd's Notes are for laymen, pastors, teachers, small-group leaders, and participants, as well as the classroom student. Enrich your personal study or quiet time. Shorten your class or small-group preparation time as you gain valuable insights into the truths of God's Word that you can pass along to your students or group members.

DESIGNED FOR QUICK ACCESS

Those with time constraints will especially appreciate the timesaving features built in the *Shepherd's Notes*. All features are intended to aid a quick and concise encounter with the heart of the message.

Concise Commentary. Galatians is replete with characters, places, and events. Short sections provide quick "snapshots" of the apostle Paul's narratives and arguments, highlighting important points and other information.

Outlined Text. A comprehensive outline covers the entire text of Galatians. This is a valuable feature for following the narrative's flow, allowing for a quick, easy way to locate a particular passage.

Shepherd's Notes. These summary statements appear at the close of every key section of the narrative. While functioning in part as a quick summary, they also deliver the essence of the message presented in the sections they cover.

Icons. Various icons in the margin highlight recurring themes in Galatians, aiding in selective searching or tracing of those themes.

Sidebars and Charts. These specially selected features provide additional background information to your study or preparation. These include definitions as well as cultural, historical, and biblical insights.

Maps. These are placed at appropriate places in the book to aid your understanding and study of a text or passage.

Questions to Guide Your Study. These thought-provoking questions and discussion starters are designed to encourage interaction with the truth and principles of God's Word.

DESIGNED TO WORK FOR YOU

Personal Study. Using the *Shepherd's Notes* with a passage of Scripture can enlighten your study and take it to a new level. At your fingertips is information that would require searching several volumes to find. In addition, many points of application occur throughout the volume, contributing to personal growth.

Teaching. Outlines frame the text of Galatians and provide a logical presentation of the message. Capsule thoughts designated as "Shepherd's Notes" provide summary statements for presenting the essence of key points and events. Application icons point out personal application of the message of Galatians. Historical Context and Cultural Context icons indicate where background information is supplied.

Group Study. *Shepherds Notes* can be an excellent companion volume for gaining a quick but accurate understanding of the message of a Bible book. Each group member can benefit by having his or her own copy. The *Shepherd's Notes* format accommodates the study of or the tracing of themes throughout Galatians. Leaders may use its flexible features to prepare for group sessions, or use them during group sessions. The Questions to Guide Your Study can spark discussion of the key points and truths of the message of Galatians.

LIST OF MARGIN ICONS USED IN GALATIANS

Shepherd's Notes. Placed at the end of each section, a capsule statement that provides the reader with the essence of the message of that section.

Old Testament Reference. Used when the writer refers to Old Testament Scripture passages that are related to or have a bearing on the passage's understanding or interpretation.

New Testament Reference. Used when the writer refers to New Testament passages that are related to or have a bearing on the passage's understanding or interpretation.

Historical Background. To indicate historical, cultural, geographical, or biographical information that sheds light on the understanding or interpretation of a passage.

Personal Application. Used when the text provides a personal or universal application of truth.

Word Picture. Indicates that the meaning of a specific word or phrase is illustrated so as to shed light on it.

Galatians ranks as one of the most important books in the New Testament. It is crucial for understanding the apostle Paul. Written in the heat of one of his most important battles, it gives us vital insights into the mind and heart of the apostle. Galatians is basic for understanding Christian faith. It probes the question, "How does a person come into a right relationship with God?"

This letter is pivotal in the unfolding of Christian history. Fifteen hundred years after Paul wrote this letter, a German monk named Martin Luther found it to be his guide out of bondage into Christian freedom. Luther loved this letter so much he called it his *Katie von Bora*—his wife!

Galatians is pertinent for today, for Christianity is still threatened from one side by legalistic cults and self-righteous pride and from the other by those who would turn Christian liberty into license.

A close look at the letter in its original setting will help us to understand its message and apply its truth to our lives.

AUTHOR

Except for one or two extreme critics of an earlier period, no one questions that Paul the apostle was the author of Galatians. Not only did he give us his name at the beginning (1:1) and near the end (5:2); he devoted the first two chapters to describing his experience as apostle to the Gentiles. No one but Paul fits the description given there.

Some important characteristics of the apostle shine through the letter. He was a preacher who stated his theology against a background of intense personal experience. He received his message by revelation of Jesus Christ (1:12). He faithfully communicated this revelation with passion and power. Deeply spiritual, he was also thoroughly human. He expressed surprise (1:6), disappointment, and fear (4:11). He was perplexed (4:20). He showed anger and impatience (1:9; 2:14; 5:12; 6:17).

AUDIENCE

In the third century B.C, wandering tribes of Gauls from Europe entered the area. They fought with the inhabitants until they were overcome and confined to the region that came to be known as the kingdom of Galatia, after the name "Gaul." Galatia continued to be an independent kingdom until the death of King Amyntas in 25 B.C At this time the area came under Roman control.

Paul addressed his letter "to the churches of Galatia" (1:2) and called the readers "Galatians" (3:1). Where is Galatia, and who are the Galatians? There are two possible answers to this question and much disagreement as to which is correct.

First, Galatia was a mountainous territory in central Asia Minor (modern-day Turkey). It included the cities of Pessinus, Ancyra (Ankara, capital of Turkey today), and Tavium.

The Romans expanded the province of Galatia southward to include parts of Lycaonia, Phrygia, and Pisidia. Thus the name Galatia could mean the old kingdom in the northern highlands or the Roman province that included other territory in the south.

Throughout much of Christian history it was thought that Paul addressed his letter to territorial or ethnic Galatia, the area of the old Gallic kingdom. This view is called the North Galatia Theory. It assumes that Paul did missionary work in North Galatia (Acts 16:6) on his second missionary journey and at the beginning of the third journey (Acts 18:23). Some commentators, mostly European scholars, continue to hold to this view today.

Other commentators, including most British and American scholars, prefer the South Galatia Theory, although they admit there are some good arguments on both sides. In this view, Galatia refers to the Roman province, particularly the southern part where Paul on his first missionary journey founded churches at Antioch of Pisidia, Iconium, Lystra, and Derbe.

Advocates of the North Galatia Theory point out that in the Book of Acts, Luke did not speak of Antioch, Lystra, Derbe, and Iconium as towns of Galatia, so Paul would not likely do so. They assert that Galatia must be a geographical term because Luke used geographical designations such as Pisidia, Phrygia, and Lycaonia in Acts. Furthermore, they say, the people of the southern area would not be called Galatians, even when their province was called Galatia.

Proponents of the South Galatia Theory say that in his other writings Paul spoke in terms of Roman provinces, not geographical territories. They also feel that the isolated, mountainous area of north Galatia would not likely be the scene of activity by the Judaizers who worked against Paul. Paul spoke of Barnabas as one well known to the Galatians, and we know that Barnabas accompanied Paul on his campaign in the southern territory. Finally, they contend, there is no clear evidence that Paul was ever in the territory of North Galatia. It is more reasonable, they say, to think in terms of the area where we have abundant records of Paul's activity.

The evidence for the South Galatia Theory seems more convincing, although not irrefutable. In either case, the interpretation of the letter is not changed. The major point of difference would be in the dating.

DATE OF WRITING

The North Galatia Theory would require a later date for the writing, since the supposed work in that area began later than in the south. Those who hold that view date the writing during the third missionary journey, possibly from Ephesus around A.D. 55.

The South Galatia Theory permits, but does not require, an earlier date. Some scholars believe it was written before the Jerusalem Council, described in Acts 15, because it does not mention that momentous decision regarding ministry to the Gentiles. If it were written before that council, it would be dated around A.D. 49 and would be the earliest of Paul's letters. This early date would make it easier to understand Peter's inconsistent attitude toward fellowship with Gentiles (Gal. 2:11–14).

Others believe that the theology expressed in Galatians is closer to that found in Romans and 1 and 2 Corinthians, which were written later. They maintain that an earlier writing would reflect more of the doctrinal concerns seen in 1 and 2 Thessalonians, which were written earlier. They, whether North or South Galatianists, date the letter around A.D. 55. The following chart contrasts the two views.

North Galatia Theory	South Galatia Theory
1. Paul's first missionary journey	1. Paul's first missionary journey
2. Jerusalem Council	2. Writing of Galatians
3. Paul's second missionary journey	3. Jerusalem Council
4. Writing of Galatians	4. Paul's second missionary journey

OCCASION AND PURPOSE

Occasion. Paul had been as devoted to the Law and the traditions of Judaism as anyone, but he was the first to see fully and clearly that these things were not necessary. God led him to preach salvation to the Gentiles, and he quickly saw that faith in Christ, not works of the Law, made a person righteous.

There were other Christians besides Paul who had been Pharisees. When Paul and Barnabas returned from the first missionary journey, they found some of these at Antioch telling the believers that circumcision was essential for salvation (Acts 15:1). This led to a conference at Jerusalem where, again, converted Pharisees urged obedience to the Law of Moses (Acts 15:5). The council, under the leadership of James and Peter, decreed that Gentile believers were not to be burdened with the Jewish Law. Their letter to this effect indicated that the Judaizers had already been active not only at Antioch, but throughout Syria and in Cilicia (Acts 15:23–24).

Purpose. With that background in mind, it is easy to understand what must have happened in the Galatian churches. Paul had come to Galatia with the good news of salvation in Christ. Paul had three closely related purposes in mind when he wrote Galatians:

Christians today sometimes forget that the first believers were Jews. They continued to be Jews after they became Christians. At first it did not dawn on them that one could be a Christian and not be a Jew. Only gradually did they come to appreciate that the gospel provided a radically new and different basis for right relationship with God. It was hard for them to conceive of a person who was in right standing with God but was not circumcised and did not keep the requirements of the Jewish Law.

1. He was defending his authority as an apostle against those who claimed otherwise.

2. He was stating, explaining, and proving the gospel message.

3. He was applying the gospel message to daily living by the power of the Holy Spirit.

Most of those Galatians who believed were Gentiles. They had no background in Judaism. They found salvation and freedom in Christ. But when Paul left the area, his opponents, the Judaizers, were not far behind. Soon the Galatian believers were led astray (Gal. 1:6). Like most new converts, they were eager to do right and to prove their faithfulness. When these new teachers came, claiming the authority of the Jerusalem apostles, their appeal was irresistible. The new Christians were ready to add circumcision and the Law to their faith in Christ.

To Paul, this was a most serious crisis. If this were allowed to go unchecked, Christianity would lapse into being a cult of Judaism. Freedom in Christ would be exchanged for a new kind of slavery. The gospel would be hopelessly distorted. Strong, decisive action was called for. The apostle sat down and, under the leadership of the Holy Spirit, wrote an impassioned restatement of the gospel of grace.

STRUCTURE OF THE LETTER

In recent years, New Testament scholars have devoted much attention to the structure and form of the Pauline letters, analyzing their literary features and comparing them with other letters that have survived from the Hellenistic world. By the time of Paul, letter writing in the Roman Empire had developed into a fine art among the professional clientele of the educated elite.

Generally, Paul's epistles do seem to follow the normal pattern of the Hellenistic letter, the basic form of which consists of five major sections.

OUTLINE

A quick look at the text of Galatians will show that it fits this pattern rather neatly with one exception: There is no thanksgiving or blessing. Otherwise, using this structure, we could lay out this structural outline for Galatians:

1. Opening (1:1–5);
2. Body (1:6–4:31);
3. Ethical instruction/exhortation (5:1–6:10); and,
4. Closing (6:11–18).

CONTENTS AND LITERARY STYLE

Contents. The message of Galatians can be summed up in one key verse: "It is for freedom that Christ has set us free. Stand firm, then, and do not let yourselves be burdened again by a yoke of slavery" (5:1).

The Book is composed of three sections of two chapters each. Chapters 1–2 give Paul's personal history as the basis for his appeal to the Galatians. Chapter 3–4 give his theological, or doctrinal, appeal. Chapters 5–6 give his challenge to spiritual living.

The argument is strong and thorough. Paul detailed the history of his apostleship to counter the false claims of the Judaizers (1:1–2:14). He developed his doctrine of salvation by grace from many angles, beginning with his own personal testimony (2:15–21). He then appealed to the Galatians' own experience (3:1–5).

1. Opening (sender, addressee, greeting);
2. Thanksgiving or blessing (often with prayer of intercession, well wishes, or personal greetings);
3. The burden of the letter (including citation of classical sources and arguments);
4. Parenesis (ethical instruction, exhortation); and
5. Closing (mention of personal plans, mutual friends, benediction.

Next he turned to the Old Testament, showing Abraham to be the prototype of justification by faith (3:6–18). He went on to discuss Law and promise, showing that the role of the Law is temporary, while faith in God's Word is permanent (3:19–29). He warned against returning to bondage and reminded the Galatians of his experience with them (4:8–20). He climaxed this doctrinal section with an allegory drawn from the life of Abraham, illustrating spiritual truth with historical events—an approach much used in the ancient world (4:21–31). On this basis, Paul made his practical appeal.

Literary Style. The style of the letter is interesting and impressive. Paul used many colorful figures of speech. There are numerous rhetorical questions. Personal references give the letter warmth. By using the first person plural "we," Paul identified with his readers. Although we do not know the effect the letter had in Galatia, the fact that it was preserved and treasured in the churches would indicate that it was effective in its mission. Paul's skill as a communicator is evident throughout.

Galatians is really a book about the relationship between persons and God. How can a man or woman find peace with God and live in harmony with Him? The answer is, "Through faith in Jesus Christ." The problem comes when we try to add other requirements. There is a strong tendency for people to add other requirements or to substitute them for faith in Christ altogether. Although circumcision may not be an issue today, other things are.

THE MEANING OF GALATIANS FOR TODAY

At first glance, the Book of Galatians seems to be an argument against circumcision and other requirements of Jewish legalism. If that is all we see, it will not seem very meaningful for contemporary life. Those issues were settled long ago. The key to reading Galatians in the present tense is to see the larger, basic issues.

It is significant that almost every cult and distorted form of religion involves some kind of legalism. And even within the major Christian churches, there is always the danger that we will substitute our own requirements for God's way of redemption. Why is legalism such a persistent danger?

For one thing, legalism appeals to pride, while faith in Christ requires repentance and humility. As long as religion can be reduced to regulations, those who try hard can feel good about their accomplishments. To say, "My only hope is the grace of God in Christ" is hard on the ego.

Legalism is also more natural to human experience. It puts religion on the same basis as most of the rest of our experiences, which are transactions involving effort and competition.

Legalism is also easier to manage than grace. If righteousness can be reduced to certain well-defined duties, a person can do these more easily than he can exercise a life-changing faith. Christian freedom requires the inner motivation of the Holy Spirit, but legalism provides the external force of laws and punishments. Those who administer the regulations can control other people, as many cult leaders do, by defining the rules their way.

Finally, legalism seems safer than grace. Freedom is dangerous. If matters are left up to the conscience of the individual, there is more danger of confusion and mistakes. Insecure people fear that life will get out of control, and they feel better if someone with authority will tell them what to do.

Galatians speaks not only to the endless danger of legalism; it also speaks to another trend in modern life—the abuse of freedom and the absence of moral order. Legalists are right in that control is needed. They are wrong about where the control must come from. Outward restrictions of the Law are mostly ineffective in creating moral living. Such morality can only come from within as persons are energized by the Spirit of God.

QUESTIONS TO GUIDE YOUR STUDY

1. How do we know that Paul is the author of Galatians?
2. What is the debate over north or south Galatia?
3. Why did Paul write this letter to the Galatian Christians? Why is its message relevant to us today?
4. Describe the structure of the Book of Galatians. How does Paul present his arguement.

The Life and Ministry of Paul

Major Events	Biblical Records		Possible Dates
	Acts	Galatians	
Birth			A.D. 1
Conversion	9:1–25	1:11–17	33
First Jerusalem visit	9:26–30	1:18–20	36
Famine	11:25–30	2:1–10?	46
First missionary journey	13:1 to 14:28		47–48
Apostolic council in Jerusalem	15:1–29	2:1–10?	49
Second missionary journey	15:36 to 18:21		
Letter to the Galatians			53–55
Third missionary journey	18:23 to 21:6		53–57
Letters to the Corinthians			55
Arrest and imprisonment in Jerusalem and Caesarea	21:8 to 26:32		57
Imprisonment in Rome	27:1 to 28:30		60–62
Letter to the Ephesians			60–62
Death			67

"What Did Paul Look Like?"

The word *Paul* literally means "small" or "little." The earliest physical description we have of Paul comes from *The Acts of Paul and Thecla*, a second-century apocryphal writing that describes the apostle as "a man of small stature, with a bald head and crooked legs, in a good state of body; for now he appeared like a man, and now he had the face of an angel." [E. Hennecke and W. Schneemelcher, eds., *New Testament Apocrypha* (Philadelphia: Westminster, 1964), 2:354.] Although written many years after his death, those words may well reflect an authentic tradition about Paul's likeness.

THE APOSTOLIC SALUTATION (1:1–5)

When Paul wrote to believers, he began his letters with the standard form for letters of the that day. Letters in the first century, whether Jewish or Greek, usually began with a salutation that included three parts: name of sender, name of the recipient, and a formula of greeting. (See "Structure of the Letter" in Introduction.)

But Paul's letters were more than ordinary letters. They were inspired statements of the gospel and impassioned defenses of his call and mission as an apostle. Even in the greeting of each letter he stated his deepest convictions and outlined key points in his message. This is especially true in these first verses of Galatians.

The Sender (vv. 1–2a)

The writer identifies himself as "Paul, an apostle."

In the New Testament, *apostle* applies primarily to the Twelve whom Jesus called as His first disciples. One of the requirements of being an apostle in this sense is that the person be a witness of Jesus' resurrection.

In this salutation Paul introduces what will be an important theme of Galatians. He is an apostle—literally: "not from men, neither through man." Rather, his call and commission were directly through Jesus Christ and God the Father who had raised Him from death.

The Recipient (v. 12b)

In the New Testament we find the word *church* used in two senses. Sometimes it refers to the whole company of all the redeemed of all ages and places, the place, the body of Christ

"So glorious is his redemption that it should ravage us with wonder."
—John Calvin
[Taken from Calvin, CNT 11]

extended throughout time as well as space. More often, however, Paul uses the word *church* in Galatians to refer to local congregations of baptized believers who regularly met for worship and witness.

The Greeting (vv. 3–5)

Galatians begins and ends with "grace." Verses 3–5, which form the closing part of the one-sentence (in Greek) salutation, are no doubt taken from a standard formula of community prayer with its liturgical opening, "Grace and peace," and its concluding affirmation, "Amen!" In fact, each of Paul's letters in the New Testament begins with a reference to "grace and peace." But for Paul this is more than a liturgical formula. "Grace and peace" summarize God's way with human beings. Grace is God's undeserved kind intention carried out on behalf of sinful human beings. Peace is the result of grace received.

Paul attributes this double blessing to a single source—the one God who knows Himself and reveals Himself as Father, Son, and Holy Spirit. Grace is seen (v. 4) in Christ's giving Himself over to death for our sins. Peace results as He delivers us out of this present evil world.

"The evil present age" Paul speaks of is the context in which God's purpose of salvation is now unfolding. Christ has rescued us from this evil present age through justifying us by faith and pouring out His Spirit in our lives. But while Christ has rescued us from this evil age, He has not taken us out of it.

Paul concludes his greeting with an expression of praise and worship—a doxology: "To whom be glory for ever and ever. Amen." Its inclusion is no mere formality. Paul's point here is that to contemplate who God is and what He has done in Christ Jesus is to fall on our knees in worship, thanksgiving, and praise.

NO OTHER GOSPEL (1:6–10)

The Crisis in Galatia (vv. 6–7)

Paul usually began his letters with words of appreciation for his readers. Even for the Corinthians (1 Cor. 1:4–9) whose carelessness had created numerous problems, Paul had words of praise and commendation. Not so for the churches in Galatia.

The transition from his greeting to the body of the letter is so abrupt as to be almost jarring. Paul marveled at what the Galatians were doing. Olaf M. Norlie translates this phrase as, "I am dumfounded." The verb tense implies that Paul is in a continual state of being dumfounded at what the Galatians had done (Herschel H. Hobbs, *Galatians* (Dallas: Word, 1978), 23). He wanted them to know how shocked he was at the new turn they had taken, as if astonishment would startle them into awareness. He also let them know in no uncertain terms that the course they had taken was wrong.

They were "deserting the one" who had called them to the grace of Christ, and instead turning to a "different gospel." Paul contrasted the message of the Judaizers with the gospel. It seemed to be another gospel, but it was so different that it was not a gospel at all. The Greek language has two words for "another." The one used here means "different." In turning to legalism, the Galatians had deserted the one who called them, God Himself. The grace of Christ was their rightful allegiance, and they had abandoned this.

"Deserting"

In verse 6, Paul told the Galatians that they were "deserting" God. The word *desert* is a striking word. Literally, it means "to bring to another place." Historically, the word was used of desertion or revolt in a military or political defection. It often expressed the idea of a change in one's religion, philosophy, or morals. By using this word, Paul was calling the Galatians spiritual turncoats!

Anathema! is actually a Greek word that has been carried over into English. It was used to translate a Hebrew word meaning "devoted to God for destruction." It denotes something that is totally rejected by God—such as idols and valuable goods that Israelites captured in battle with their enemies—and which they were commanded to destroy.

What the Galatians failed to realize was the decisive character of who Jesus was and what He had accomplished in His atoning death on the cross. To Christ's completed work, they wanted to add something that, from their own perspective, seemed so right, so reasonable, and so religious. They were not aware that adding *anything* to grace changes grace to something other than grace and undermines the way God has provided for sinful human beings to be made right with Him.

The Counterfeit Gospel: Anathema! (vv. 8–9)

In these verses Paul paints two future scenarios in order to drive home point. He says, let's suppose I, Paul, came to you at some future date and preached a new and different gospel to you. If I did that, let me be eternally condemned. Or suppose an angel from heaven came to you and preached a different gospel. Let him, too, be eternally condemned. The fact that Paul issued this condemnation in the strongest words possible and then repeated it for emphasis makes this one of the harshest statements in the entire New Testament. The word translated "condemned" is the word *anathema!*

Herschel Hobbs observes that Paul's words sound overly harsh to modern ears. In an age of relativism, Paul's stance here is far from being politically correct. But Hobbs says, "No sane person wants a banker who says that two plus two equals three. . . . We do not want a pharmacist who just throws together any drugs which may suit his fancy. We want him to follow exactly the doctor's prescription. This is true narrow-mindedness. We commend this quality in matters of lesser importance—finances and health. But many condemn it in matters of religion," (Hobbs, *Galatians*, 27).

Paul's Motive for Ministry (v. 10)

Paul says that his strong reaction to the direction the Galatians are taking is not motivated by his desire to win their approval. He may have at one time been motivated by human approval—but no longer. One who becomes a servant of Jesus Christ sets his heart on pleasing Christ first—and lets the chips fall where they may.

■ *In the first ten verses of Galatians, Paul*
■ *moves from formal greeting to an impassioned*
■ *warning that the Galatian Christians were on*
■ *the brink of a course of action that would be*
■ *destructive to them and to other churches.*

GOD'S REVELATION TO PAUL (1:11–17)

Having stated the problem, Paul now begins to develop his argument. His first line of argument is personal history, contained in the first two chapters of Galatians.

Paul's Call from Above (vv. 11–12)

These two verses introduce the theme that Paul alluded to in the introduction and will more fully develop in the following narrative—that the gospel he preached to the Galatians was not devised by any human source, but came directly from God Himself—a "revelation from Jesus Christ." To impress the truth of this upon his readers, Paul introduced it with a solemn disclosure formula: "I want you to know."

The phrase translated "according to man" relates back to and encompasses the twin negatives found in 1:1, "*not* from men *nor* by man." Paul's apostleship and his gospel was neither *from* nor *by* any human source.

Revelation

Revelation is an unveiling or a disclosure. It "refers to God's actions of making Himself known to humans. This action is necessary because humans, being limited, are unable to know God by their own ability of discovery. Just as dogs or cats cannot investigate their master, and if they could, would not really understand him, so humans do not have the capability of finding God by their own effort. Because God loves His human creatures and wants to have fellowship with them, He has therefore made Himself known." [Millard J. Erickson from *Foundations for Biblical Interpretation*]

Paul then elaborated this denial by adding two additional negative qualifications concerning his gospel's nonhuman character: <u>he neither received it through tradition</u> nor <u>was taught it through the ordinary means</u> of instruction. These two additional denials both point to the same reality and are nearly identical in meaning.

Having asserted that the gospel was not of human origin and that it came through a direct revelation to him by Christ, Paul offers five pieces of evidence in support of his claim.

Evidence	Passage
1. Nothing in Paul's religious background could account for his acceptance of the gospel.	1:13–17
2. Paul was not commissioned by the Jerusalem church.	1:18–20
3. Those Paul formerly persecuted glorified God because of the change wrought in him.	1:21–24
4. Paul's apostolic work was recognized by church leaders at Jerusalem.	2:1–10
5. Paul defended the gospel against Peter's vacillation at Antioch.	2:11–14

Following this extensive historical section, Paul summarizes the central theme of his letter (2:15–21) and then reminds the Galatians of how God had worked among them at his first preaching of the gospel in their midst (3:1–5). Thus the entire historical section of the letter moves from <u>Paul the persecutor to Paul the preacher</u>. It is the record of the gospel's movement from Damascus to Galatia.

Paul's Life before Christ (vv. 13–14)

Paul's main point in these verses is to show that there was nothing in his religious background and his life before his conversion that could have prepared him for a positive response to the gospel. Quite the contrary. His early career and lifestyle were shaped by a confident attachment to the strictest traditions of Judaism, which in turn had led him to take up arms against believers in Jesus.

Paul's use of the term *church* stands in marked contrast to his earlier address to the "churches in Galatia." Clearly, here he has in mind the Church universal, the body of Christ, which is the company of all the redeemed throughout the world.

■ *Paul's background did not explain his con-*
■ *version. For such a Jewish leader to change*
■ *would require divine intervention. Paul's*
■ *changed life was proof of the validity of his*
■ *experience, "a revelation from Jesus Christ."*

Paul's Conversion and Calling (vv. 15–17)

Paul described the sovereign initiative of God in terms of three distinct acts, all of which were according to God's good pleasure:

1. *Paul was set apart.*
2. *Paul was called.* Not only was Paul chosen from eternity and set apart from his mother's womb; he was also called by God at a specific point in his life.
3. *God revealed His Son through Paul.* Many commentators believe that Paul was here referring to his encounter with the risen

Paul used the word we translate as "set apart" also in Rom. 1:1, where he describes himself as being "set apart for the gospel of God." Literally, the word means "to determine beforehand." Paul had in mind something that was even prior to the occasion of his birth—God's eternal predestination and good pleasure by which He chose us in Christ before the creation of the world (Eph. 1:4).

Arabia

The Arabia of Paul's day was not identical with the boundaries of contemporary Saudi Arabia. This was a vast territory lying between the Red Sea on the southwest and the Persian Gulf and Euphrates River on the northeast.

Christ on the road to Damascus. Thus, "to reveal his Son in me" is another way of describing the call Paul received at this decisive juncture of his life.

PAUL'S FIRST VISIT TO JERUSALEM (1:18–24)

Paul now begins a second line of defense, a tightly woven alibi designed to show that his contacts with the Jerusalem church were such that he could not possibly have been dependent on the Jerusalem church or its leaders for his authority or for that portion of revelation imparted directly to him by Christ.

Following his conversion, Paul didn't go to Jerusalem. Rather, he went to Arabia.

Some have suggested that Paul went to Arabia to preach the gospel. Luke tells us that he began preaching in Damascas immediately following his conversion. Others believe he went to Arabia for a retreat—for time to study the Scriptures, to meditate on them, and to pray. Such a time was needed for Paul to assimilate his encounter with Christ on the road to Damascas.

These reasons for going to Arabia are not mutually exclusive. Both may be true.

Paul Meets with Peter (vv. 18–19)

Paul says he went to Jerusalem "to get acquainted with Peter."

The reference to "three years" is not precise. It doesn't necessarily mean that Paul spent three years in Arabia. It does imply that there were at least three years between his conversion and his journey to Jerusalem. By this time, the gospel imparted to him by the Lord would have been well assimilated.

Upon arriving in Jerusalem, Paul was a house guest of Peter. We wish we could have been a fly on the wall during their dinner conversations!

A. T. Robertson paints a possible scenario:

It is pleasant to think of them here together for two weeks in Jerusalem. Paul would naturally be the learner and let Peter tell the history of Jesus in particular as it was connected with Jerusalem. There was Bethany; here was the road of the Truumphant Entry; down there was Gethsemane, where Peter went to sleep; here Jesus was arrested; at this place the trial took place and just here Peter had denied him; and on yonder hill they crucified him; and in that tomb they buried him; lo! here was the spot where Jesus had appeared to Peter after his resurrection; in this upper room he had appeared to the disciples twice; up here on Olivet was the place where they had caught the last glimpse of him as he went up on the cloud. [A. T. Robertson, *Epochs in the Life of Paul,* (Nashville: Broadman Press, 1974), 81–2].

Paul learned historical details of Jesus' life. Peter learned from Paul what the risen Lord had imparted to Paul concerning the gospel and how it related to God's revelation prior to Christ.

An important point here is that Paul did not seek authorization of his message or validation of his ministry from Peter. He did seek a close fellowship in the things of the Lord as well as a strategic partnership in their common apostolic mission.

The only other apostle Paul met was James, the Lord's brother. Paul includes James among the other apostles, even though he was not one of the Twelve. Apparently, the term *apostle* extended to other leaders beyond the original circle.

James, the brother of Jesus

Here are seven fairly well established facts about James.

James is one of the most important and fascinating characters in the history of the early church, although there is much about him we do not know. However, the following facts are firmly established.

1. James was not a follower of Jesus during His earthly life.

2. Jesus made a special resurrection appearance to James (1 Cor. 15:7).

3. James became a member of the church at Jerusalem.

4. James quickly rose to a position of leadership within the Jerusalem church.

5. James is known as the "Just," obviously because of his personal piety and strict observance of Jewish customs.

6. In all likelihood James wrote the general epistle that bears his name.

7. In A.D. 62 James was put to death through the conniving of the Sadducees who administered the temple.

So Help Me God! (v. 20)

Paul then asserted a solemn warning that what he was saying was the truth. The issue was so important that Paul felt he must set the record straight in the clearest possible terms: "I assure you before God that what I am writing you is no lie." He was not a secondary apostle, dependent on others for his message and, therefore, subject to their correction. His faith and calling came by revelation from Christ Himself.

A Mission to Syria and Cilicia (v. 21)

Paul left Jerusalem, according to Acts 9:26–30, because his preaching aroused the anger of the Greek-speaking Jews there. His life in danger, he went to Tarsus. He referred to the regions of Syria and Cilicia, neighboring territories that were part of the same Roman province. What was the result of Paul's ministry in these places? We cannot say for sure, but it is clear from later references in Acts that Paul's witness bore fruit in the conversion of new believers and the planting of several churches.

Reaction to Paul in Judea (vv. 22–24)

In these closing verses, Paul shifted the perspective away from his missionary activities back to the local environment around Jerusalem. Paul registered the reaction of the Jerusalem churches to his early ministry. He did this by referring to three facts: (1) his lack of personal acquaintance with the Judean churches; (2) the impression of his work that was conveyed to them; and (3) their jubilant reaction at the report of the persecutor-turned-proclaimer.

The doxology in verse 24, "And they praised God because of me" echoes the earlier doxology at the conclusion of the introduction (1:5). The first doxology is a hymn of praise for what God has done through the atoning death and triumphant resurrection of Jesus Christ. This second doxology celebrates that same victory as seen in the calling and apostolic ministry of Paul.

■ *Paul was well thought of by the Christians in*
■ *Jerusalem, but he was in no way dependent*
■ *on them. He was an apostle in his own right.*

"And all those hearing him continued to be amazed, and were saying, 'Is this not he who in Jerusalem destroyed those who called on his name, and who had come here for the purpose of bringing them bound before the priests?'" Acts 9:21 (NASB)

QUESTIONS TO GUIDE YOUR STUDY

1. Describe the crisis taking place in Galatia. What was Paul's point about the gospel the Galatians were preaching?

2. What reasons did Paul give to support his claim that his calling was independent of the other apostles?

3. What are the implications of the doctrines of election and predestination for us?

4. What was Paul's purpose for visiting Peter during his first visit to Jerusalem? What do you suppose they discussed?

GALATIANS 2

THE APOSTOLIC MESSAGE—CONFIRMATION AND CHALLENGE (2:1–21)

Chapter 2 continues Paul's defense of his commission as an apostle and of the integrity of the gospel he received directly from Jesus Christ.

The chapter divides naturally into two major sections.

Fourteen years passed. It is not clear whether Paul was counting these years from his conversion or from his first visit to Jerusalem. The latter seems a more natural interpretation of the word *then,* immediately following the account of the first visit.

In the first (2:1–10), Paul recounts an important meeting he had with the Jerusalem church—the issue of circumcision, which now dominates the appeal being made to his Galatian converts by the false teachers.

The second section (2:11–21) centers on another meeting between Peter and Paul, this time at Antioch, where again the issue of legalism threatened to disrupt the unity of the church.

PAUL'S SECOND VISIT TO JERUSALEM (2:1–10)

In these opening verses the stage is set for the drama that is about to unfold. Let us notice the event itself, the parties involved, and the motive behind Paul's action.

The Event (vv. 1–2)

Paul had established the fact that he was independent of the leaders of the church at Jerusalem. Now he proceeded to show that the leaders of the Jerusalem church approved his gospel and his mission to the Gentiles without asking him to require circumcision.

The Parties Involved (v. 2)

In the narrative that follows, there are three groups of principal actors, each of which plays a distinct role in the decision of the conference and its aftermath.

First, we have the Pauline party consisting of Barnabas, Titus, and Paul.

Second, we have the "false brothers" who agitated for Titus to become circumcised and later imported their teachings to Antioch itself.

The third party that plays a prominent role in the narrative are the leaders of the Jerusalem church—James, Peter, and John—whose prominence had given them the name "pillars."

Paul's main negotiations were with these church leaders, not with his Judaizing detractors, although the close relationship between the "pillars" and some of their more zealous disciples must have created a situation of great tension for everyone involved.

Paul's Motive (v. 2)

Paul made three important points about his motivation for his second visit to Jerusalem:

1. He insisted that he was prompted to call this meeting "in response to a revelation."

This is the same word Paul used in 1:12 which describes the revelation of the risen Christ on the road to Damascus as well as other revelations Paul had.

2. In such a setting the leaders in Jerusalem could hear with their own ears what Paul was proclaiming to the Gentiles. He wanted to reach agreement with the Jerusalem leaders on the message God had given to him.

If this message were from God, why did Paul need consensus with the Jerusalem church?

In one sense, he didn't need their approval or consensus. What God has commissioned and communicated doesn't require human approval. On the other hand, for the health and well-being of the church, what God has revealed needs to be recognized and acted on by the church. Otherwise, it will remain hidden at least for a time.

3. Thus Paul sought to resolve a crisis that could have led to a major division within the body of Christ. Paul would later say, "Let us

In this case, Paul was speaking most likely about a specific word from the Lord related to the growing rift and controversy concerning Paul's message and its reception throughout the church at large.

The Judaizers had probably painted caricatures of Paul as one who was departing from God's revelation to Israel. God's Spirit made clear to Paul, directly or through the church at Antioch, the need to sit down face to face with the leaders of the Jerusalem church.

Meeting face to face over differences is a healthy first step toward handling church conflict constructively. Hearing directly what a brother or sister is saying is far better than relying on secondhand sources of information.

1. *Infiltrated.* The idea is that of a conspiracy of error, a secret plot concocted by enemies of the faith, informants, and double agents deliberately planted to ferret out confidential information. This word can also express the idea of activity carried out for sinister purposes. Here in Galatians it points unmistakably to the unworthy motives of the false brothers.

2. *Spy.* This word means "to spy on, to destroy in a sneaky manner." This word is related to another word, *oversight*, which Paul used in a positive sense to describe pastoral authority in the governing of a New Testament congregation.

therefore make every effort to do what leads to peace and to mutual edification" (Rom. 14:19).

Titus and the False Brothers (vv. 3–5)

Verse 3 is the first mention of circumcision in the epistle. It is easy to see why the question of circumcision arose with regard to Titus. Here, in Jerusalem itself, Paul introduced a Gentile as a brother in Christ. For the ancient Hebrews, circumcision was a sign of the covenant relationship with God dating back to Abraham (Gen. 17:11–14). It was commanded of God's chosen people. Under Moses it became a requirement of the Law (Exod. 12:43–48). No wonder the Jews who were Christians had doubts about Christians who were not circumcised. Judaizers had already advanced the claim, "Unless you are circumcised . . . you cannot be saved" (Acts 15:1).

Paul emphasized that Titus was not compelled to be circumcised. The Jerusalem apostles did not require this, even though there were agitators present who tried to force the issue. Their aim, Paul said, was to undermine the freedom we have in Christ—a step that would result in bondage. Paul stood his ground to preserve the gospel for the sake of Gentile believers. Those who demanded circumcision of the Galatians were asking for something that had not been required by the apostles at Jerusalem.

Paul used two unusual words to characterize the activity of the false brothers. These words are from the world of political and military espionage, but they are applied to the conflict raging in the early church.

Perhaps Paul is making a deliberate contrast between the proper oversight of a godly pastor and the arrogant usurping of church power the false brothers had assumed for themselves.

■ *We can summarize what we have learned*
■ *about the false brothers with these four propo-*
■ *sitions:*
■ *1. They were not what they seemed to be.*
■ *2. They were secretive in their work of*
■   *disruption.*
■ *3. They carried out their destructive mission*
■   *step-by-step.*
■ *4. They demonstrated the connection between*
■   *false teaching and unworthy behavior.*

Paul and the Pillars (vv. 6–9)

Having interrupted his narration of the Jerusalem meeting to describe the intrusion of the false brothers and the Titus test case, Paul resumed the flow of his account he left off with at the end of verse 2. He drew a sharp distinction between the false brothers and the church leaders with whom he had come to Jerusalem to confer. The former were pseudo-Christians; the latter were respected leaders and dialogue partners with Paul in his strategic missionary summit.

In verse 9 we learn the identity of the "pillars." They were James, Peter, and John. Paul described them as "those reputed to be pillars." Some scholars have argued that Paul's repeated use of this expression indicates a disparagement or slighting of the authority of these church leaders. On this view, Paul would have been saying that they were reputed to be pillars, they appeared to be something, they seemed to be real leaders, but in reality their appearances were deceiving. In other words, the reality did not match the reputation.

"Reputed"

The expression "those reputed" need not carry such a derogatory meaning. It may simply mean, as the JERUSALEM BIBLE renders it, "these people who are acknowledged leaders." Here Paul may have been using a common term of respect to refer to those leaders who were men of high reputation and considered to be authorities among the believers in Jerusalem.

The basic drift of this passage (vv. 6–9), however, points not to opposition or confrontation between Paul and these leaders, but to their fundamental unity and shared task of fulfilling the Great Commission. Here, Paul rejected the idea that there is any rank or authority that determines spiritual truth. God shows no partiality toward men of reputation, and neither did Paul.

It was, however, significant to Paul that those recognized leaders did not add anything to the gospel he had received from the Lord. Therefore, the Judaizers in Galatia had no grounds for doing so.

Positive Affirmations (vv. 7–9)

Much of what Paul states in this chapter is negative in nature. However, the climax of the meeting was the mutual recognition symbolized by the right hand of fellowship and the agreed-upon division of labor in the worldwide missionary enterprise.

- *We have three affirmations in this passage.*
- One Gospel. *Paul focused on the one gospel shared by all the participants.*
- Two Apostles. *The two apostles represented the two spheres of missionary outreach.*
- Three Pillars. *The three pillars—James, Peter, and John—whose affirmation of Paul and Barnabas was crucial to the positive outcome of the conference.*

Concern for the Poor (v. 10)

This verse is a kind of postscript to the agreement Paul and Barnabas had concluded in verse 9. Paul and Barnabas were asked to remember the poor. The "poor" were the Christians in

Jerusalem who were suffering persecution and loss of property. Paul was already doing this, having brought an offering for the poor from Antioch, either on this visit or an earlier one. He was eager to continue this practice to meet a pressing need—cementing the bond of friendship between Jewish and Gentile Christians. Throughout his ministry Paul gave much attention to such relief work (1 Cor. 16:1–4; 2 Cor. 8–9; Rom. 15:25–29).

■ *The two key themes of the first ten verses of*
■ *Galatians 2 are widespread recognition of*
■ *the truth of the gospel Paul had received and*
■ *the unity of the church. This passage shows*
■ *a pattern of cooperation around the truth of*
■ *the gospel. Paul was eager to work closely*
■ *with other Christian leaders who shared*
■ *with him a common commitment to the good*
■ *news of salvation through Jesus Christ. As a*
■ *result of their conference, the apostles found*
■ *it desirable to do the work of evangelization*
■ *by a practical division of labor.*

PAUL'S CONFRONTATION WITH PETER AT ANTIOCH (2:11–14)

The Problem (vv. 11–13)
Following the consensus in Jerusalem there arose a problem centered on the issue of table fellowship. In the fast-food culture of modern Western civilization, it is difficult to appreciate the religious significance ancient peoples associated with the simple act of eating.

The problem became very clear when Peter paid a visit to Antioch. There he found Jews and

"It is a perpetual statue throughout your generations in all your dwellings: you shall not eat any fat or blood." Leviticus 3:17 (NASB)

Gentiles enjoying unbroken fellowship, including a common meal.

This was revolutionary, for Jews simply did not eat with Gentiles. The Law did not specifically forbid it, but it did impose restrictions on diet that would exclude Jews from a Gentile table. Developments in Jewish history had caused them to take extreme measures to avoid contaminating their way of life with Gentile contacts. There were traditional Jewish restrictions against the eating of unclean food, including the consumption of pork, eating food offered to idols, and partaking of meat from which the blood had not been properly drained in accordance with the Law of Moses (Lev. 3:17; 7:26–27; 17:10–14).

The agreement worked out earlier at Jerusalem said that Gentiles did not have to assume the burden of the Jewish law. It did not say that Jews could be free from it. It approved sending missionaries to the Gentiles, but it said nothing about close fellowship with them. Peter accepted the open fellowship of the congregation at Antioch and joined in.

"Hypocrisy"

The word translated "hypocrisy" comes from the world of the theater, where it refers to the act of wearing a mask or playing a part in a drama. Negatively, it came to mean pretense, insincerity, acting in a fashion that belies one's true convictions.

But the other Jewish believers were also interested in what was going on at Antioch. James himself did not come, but some of his associates did. Their presence, and perhaps their reaction, caused Peter to fear the circumcision party. He withdrew from the group meals. Worse, the other Jews joined him in his hypocrisy. Even Barnabas was swept along by their hypocritical behavior.

The Protest (v. 14)
What happened at Antioch must have been a severe blow to Christian fellowship. Paul acted quickly and decisively. He opposed Peter to his

face because Peter was clearly in the wrong. He confronted Peter in the presence of the whole congregation since the whole congregation was involved in what he was doing, and the principle was vital for all concerned. He pointed out Peter's inconsistency.

Peter was formally holding to Jewish law, but he was actually living much like the Gentiles. It was wrong for him, then, to expect Gentiles to live up to a way of life that he did not support by his own behavior. Or, as Paul put it, Peter was "not acting in line with the truth of the gospel."

There are three practical truths we can apply from this passage to the life of the church today.

1. *Great leaders can be in error.* There was every reason for Peter to resist the pressure to compromise his convictions in the face of pressure. He had been in the intimate circle of Jesus' closest disciples. He was a primary witness to the resurrection. Yet, in a moment of crisis he failed, and the force of his example led many others astray as well. May God help us to test every message we hear by the touchstone of His Word and save us from exalting any human leader above the clear voice of God.

2. *God's grace means no second-class Christians.* The withdrawal of Jewish believers from table fellowship with their Gentile brothers and sisters precipitated a serious breach within the church at Antioch. Racism of any brand within any culture is incompatible with the truth of the gospel. Later in Galatians (3:26–29) Paul spelled out the implications of Christian unity in

"Acting in line with"

This phrase is actually only one word (*orthopodein*) in the Greek text. Literally, it means "to walk with straight feet." Paul was saying that Peter was not "walking a straight course." Elsewhere in his letters Paul had much to say about the importance of the Christian's "walk" (Eph. 4:1, 17; Col. 1:10; 2:6; Rom. 13:13). And later in Galatians Paul also admonished his readers to "keep in step with the Spirit" (Gal. 5:25).

terms of the promise of grace fulfilled in Jesus Christ. Any religious system or theology that denies this truth stands in opposition to the "new creation" God is bringing into being. The body of Christ is based not on caste, color, or social condition, but on grace alone.

3. *Standing for the gospel can be a lonely business.* When the crisis became more intense, Barnabas sided with Peter in the confrontation with Paul. The Apostle to the Gentiles stood alone on behalf of the gospel. Throughout church history others have done the same. Thank God for those brave warriors of the faith who did not flinch in the hour of temptation—who refused to flirt with the false gods of their age and thus have passed on to us a goodly heritage of courage and faith.

■ *This section centers on the issue of table fel-*
■ *lowship. Paul publicly confronted and*
■ *rebuked Peter, pointing out Peter's inconsis-*
■ *tency and hypocrisy regarding the issue.*
■ *Peter was formally holding to Jewish law,*
■ *but he was actually living much like the Gen-*
■ *tiles, who did not hold to the Law. It was*
■ *wrong for him, then, to expect Gentiles to*
■ *live up to a way of life that he did not support*
■ *by his own behavior.*

THE PRINCIPLE: JUSTIFICATION BY FAITH (2:15–21)

In this concluding section of chapter 2, Paul brings to a conclusion the historical argument he has been pursuing and launches into the doctrinal exposition that will cover the next two chapters.

These seven verses contain some of the most compressed language found anywhere in Paul's epistles. Here Paul sets forth his main point—his big idea—that he wants to impress upon the Galatians: *Acceptance with God is effected through a simple act of trust in Jesus Christ and not through anything else.*

The Doctrine Declared (vv. 15–16)

In these verses Paul introduces three expressions that encompass the idea of the believer's justification by faith: *justification, the works of the Law,* and *faith in Christ.* Paul uses each of these for the first time in his letter.

Justification. In its most basic meaning, justification is the declaration that somebody is right. Justification should not be confused with forgiveness, which is the fruit of justification. Neither should it be confused with atonement, which is the basis of justification. Rather, it is the favorite verdict of God, the righteous Judge, that one who formerly stood condemned has now been granted a new status at the bar of divine justice.

The works of the Law. The Law Paul usually refers to is the specific requirements God gave to Israel through Moses. Paul's argument here is that the nature of the Law is such that it cannot produce a right relationship with God. As Paul will show in Galatians 3, the Law was given by God to play a special role in leading persons to Christ, who is the "end of the Law" (Rom. 10:4).

Faith in Christ. Paul speaks of faith as essential for justification. Faith is the necessary human response to what God has objectively

Martin Luther on the doctrine of justification by faith:

For the issue before us is grave and vital; it involves the death of the Son of God, who, by the will and command of the Father, became flesh, was crucified, and died for the sins of the world. If faith yields on this point, the death of the Son of God will be in vain. Then it is only a fable that Christ is the Savior of the world. Then God is a liar, for he has not lived up to his promises. Therefore our stubbornness on this issue is pious and holy; for by it we are striving to preserve the freedom we have in Christ Jesus and to keep the truth of the gospel. If we lose this, we lose God, Christ, all the promises, faith, righteousness, and eternal life.

—Martin Luther [Taken from LW 26.90–91].

"For it is by His unmerited favor through faith that you have been saved; it is not by anything that you have done, it is the gift of God."
Eph. 2:8 (Williams)

accomplished on the cross of Christ. At the same time we must recognize the instrumental character of such faith. Paul always tells us that we are saved "by" faith, not "on account of" faith. We must guard against the temptation to turn faith itself into one of the "works of the Law." Saving faith is a gift from God, never a mere human possibility (Eph. 2:8–9). Faith is not an achievement that earns salvation any more than circumcision is. Rather, faith is the evidence of saving grace manifested in the renewal of the heart by the Holy Spirit.

■ *Here Paul sets forth his big idea that he*
■ *wants to impress upon the Galatians: Accep-*
■ *tance with God is effected through a simple*
■ *act of trust in Jesus Christ and not through*
■ *anything else.*

Objections Answered (vv. 17–20)

These verses take us back to the troubles in the fractured church at Antioch. We may have in Paul's coded language an actual piece of the debate that raged in Antioch.

The first objection: "If, while we seek to be justified in Christ, it becomes evident that we ourselves are sinners, does that mean that Christ promotes sin?" Paul's response is, "Absolutely not!" It is one of the strongest exclamations in his vocabulary. It is not Christ who causes people to be sinners.

The fact that Jewish Christians now shared table fellowship with Gentile believers did not make them sinners. Rather, this was an expression of the Christian freedom that was theirs through the righteousness of faith.

In verse 18 Paul points his finger of blame at those who try to establish their legal righteousness, as Peter did, by going back to the Law after they had already recognized the futility of the Law.

The second objection: By displacing the Law as the proper channel for a right standing before God, had not Paul undermined the very basis for living a righteous life? Had he left no place for the practical outworking of faith in the life of the believer?

Paul uses four theses (statements from v. 20) to refute the second objection to his doctrine of justification by faith:

1. "Through the law I died to the law so that I might live for God." When Paul says that he died to the Law, he was referring to nothing less than the God-given commandments and decrees contained in Old Testament Scriptures. However, he is not saying that the Law of God had lost all meaning or relevance for the Christian believer. Rather, he is saying that his relationship to self, sin, world, and Law had been so altered by his union with Christ that they no longer controlled, dominated, or defined his existence.

The Law is the instrument of a sinner's death. But the sinner's death is not sufficient to create a right relationship with a holy God. Only God Himself, as man, can accomplish that.

So by faith, the believing sinner sees Christ's dying and recognizes that he, too, is there. His orientation to God has heretofore been either ignoring God or trying to establish right rela-

Martin Luther on Being Crucified with Christ

For we are called Christians because we may look at the Christ and say: "Dear Lord, You took all my sins upon Yourself. You became Martin, Peter, and Paul, and thus you crushed and destroyed my sin. There (on the cross) I must and will seek my sin. You have directed me to find it there. On Good Friday I clearly see my sin, but on the Day of Easter no sin is any longer to be seen. [Easter Sermon, Coburg, 7 April 530, WLS I, 182; WA 32,47 as quoted in *The Word of Life*, Thomas C. Oden, (San Francisco: Harper & Row 1989), 382.]

tionship with God through keeping God's law. But because of his sinful nature, he couldn't possibly do that.

Christ's death puts to death the self which tries to please God by keeping the Law and opens a new way—the way of faith. Faith recognizes that right relationship with God is not a human achievement but a gift from God to be received.

2. "I have been crucified with Christ." When Jewish believers witnessed the death of a sacrificial animal, such as a lamb, they recognized that this animal was dying as a consquence of their sin.

When Christian believers see the death of Christ, they see Jesus receiving the consequences of their sin. They identify with Him in His death.

3. "I no longer live, but Christ lives in me." Paul set forth in this expression his doctrine of the indwelling Christ. The indwelling of Christ does not mean that persons are delivered from their current realm of suffering, sin, and death. Christ takes up residence in the believers, sanctifying our bodies as temples of the Holy Spirit and enabling us to approach the throne of God in prayer.

Christ's death, which happened in space and time, is appropriated by the believer so it is no longer an external event but one that transforms and gives life. John Calvin says, "As long as Christ remains outside of us, and we are separated from him, all that he has suffered and done for the salvation of the human race remains useless and of no value for us." [John Calvin, *Institutes* 3.1.1, quoted in Timothy

George, *Galatians,* New American Commentary (Nashville: Broadman & Holman Publishers]

4. "The life I live in the body I live by faith in the Son of God, who loved me, and gave himself for me." While the Christian life takes place "in the flesh," it is nonetheless lived "by faith." Not only are we justified by faith; we also live by faith. This means that saving faith cannot be reduced to a one-time decision or event in the past; it is a living, dynamic reality permeating every aspect of the believer's life. The object of this faith is Jesus Christ, the Son of God, "who loved me and gave himself for me." It was the love of God—unmerited, immeasurable, infinite—that sent Jesus to the cross.

■ *Paul responded to two major objections to*
■ *his doctrine of justification by faith. His four*
■ *theses present the truths taught in verse 20.*
■ *The believer has died to the law, shares in*
■ *Christ's suffering, is the temple of the Holy*
■ *Spirit, and lives by faith.*

The Terrible Alternative (v. 21)

As we have seen, grace is the operative word in Galatians. In this concluding verse of chapter 2, Paul defends himself against the charge that by displacing the Law as a means of salvation he has thwarted God's grace. The exact opposite is true. If it were possible to obtain a right standing before God through the works of the Law, then Christ had no business dying! Was Christ a false Messiah, a common criminal whose death was merely a footnote in history? Any true Christian must tremble in horror at such a prospect.

Union with Christ

Millard Erickson identifies three dimensions to our union with Christ.

1. *The believer's union is judicial.* When God sees the believer he sees him united with Christ. He sees the believer-in-Christ as righteous, as rightly related to Him.
2. *This is a spiritual union*—a union of two spirits in which they maintain their separate identity but by which the believer's spirit is enriched by the Spirit of Christ.
3. *This is a vital union.* Jesus pictures believers as branches of the Vine—which is Himself. The life of Christ flows into and sustains the believer. *Christian Theology* (Grand Rapids: Baker Book House, 1983, 1984, 1985), pp. 952–953.

"For in thy sight, no man living is righteous."
Ps. 143:2b (ASV)

Paul says that as believers we must not persist in building again the wall that Christ has torn down. If we add works of the Law to the sacrifice of the cross, then indeed we make a mockery of Jesus' death.

Galatians 2:15–21 summarizes the themes developed thus far and introduces the theological exposition of justification by faith that Paul will pursue in chapters 3 and 4. The key verse in this section is 2:16. It contains both an appeal to Christian experience ("We, too, have put our faith in Christ Jesus") and an argument from Scripture, the quotation from Psalm 143:2 about no flesh being justified by observing the Law. Paul anticipated objections to his doctrine of justification and emphasized the life of faith to which he will return in greater detail in Galatians 5–6.

We are now ready to look at the centerpiece of Paul's doctrine of justification which he unfolds in the next two chapters.

QUESTIONS TO GUIDE YOUR STUDY

1. What was Paul's motive for returning to Jerusalem?
2. Describe the "false brothers." What was their error?
3. What was unique about Paul's status as an apostle in contrast to the Jerusalem apostles? What did he have in common with them?
4. Why did Paul rebuke Peter? Describe the issue that forced this confrontation.

SECTION INTRODUCTION: THE THEOLOGICAL ARGUMENT (3:1–5:1)

Paul's argument in this section fulfills these three purposes:

1. He wanted to show the Galatians that their contemplated return to right standing with God by keeping the Law as a method of relating to God was a contradiction of their experience (3:1–5).
2. He wanted to convince his readers that their experience had been identified with that of their forefather Abraham (3:6–9).
3. He wanted to explain the purpose and intent of the Law (3:19–25).

In chapters 3 and 4, Paul turns from the evidence of his personal experience to evidence based on theology as revealed in several doctrines he will teach. But the transition in verses 1–5 is based on an appeal to the experience of the Galatian Christians.

PROBING QUESTIONS (3:1–5)

Paul asked the Galatians a question that showed his astonishment at their deviation and directed their attention to its unreasonableness. "You foolish Galatians! Who has bewitched you?"

Paul follows this dramatic question with four rhetorical questions.

Rhetorical Question #1: "Did you receive the Spirit by observing the law, or by believing what you heard?" (v. 2)

Restated, the question is, Why should the Galatians go back to the Law when it was hearing and faith that brought the life of God into their lives? Paul's point was that the Galatians did not come to experience life in the Spirit by doing

"Bewitched"

Paul is asking the Galatians who has led them astray by the evil eye or through evil arts. This is the only occurrence of this concept in the New Testament, although this is an old and persistent concept (Deut. 28:54).

QUESTION	VERSE
1. "Did you receive the Spirit by observing the Law, or by believing what you heard?"	v. 2
2. "After beginning with the Spirit, are you now trying to attain your goal by human effort?"	v. 3
3. "Have you suffered so much for nothing—if it really was for nothing?"	v. 4
4. "Does God give you his Spirit and work miracles among you because you observe the Law, or because you believe what you heard?"	v. 5

works of the Law, but by hearing the gospel and receiving it by faith. Here Paul describes the Christian life in terms of receiving the Spirit instead of being justified. Justification is God's activity in salvation; receiving the Spirit is man's experience. Paul is focusing on the experience of his Galatian friends. (He later contrasts the Law and the Spirit in chapter 5.)

"Receive the Spirit"

The word *received* (in v. 2 and in 3:14) refers not to a self-prompted taking, but to a grateful reception of that which is offered. Therefore, the Galatians received the Holy Spirit as an unfettered gift from the sovereign God quite apart from any contribution of good works or human merit on their part.

Rhetorical Question #2: "After beginning with the Spirit, are you now trying to attain your goal by human effort?" (v. 3)

Paul next raised the contrast between the Spirit and the flesh, a basic concept in the latter part of the Book. How foolish and tragic to start out with the Spirit, the presence of God in a person's life, and to go from there to the flesh human nature as it was apart from God.

Rhetorical Question #3: "Have you suffered so much for nothing—if it really was for nothing?" (v. 4)

Paul went on to question whether the Galatians had learned anything from their experience.

The word *suffer* can mean either experience in a neutral sense or bad experience, usually the latter in the New Testament. Whichever Paul meant here, the point was, "Did you learn anything from it, or has it been wasted?" Paul was not sure that it was in vain, so he added a statement to that effect after the question.

Rhetorical Question #4: "Does God give you his Spirit and work miracles among you because you observe the law, or because you believe what you heard?" (v. 5)

The fourth and final rhetorical question concerned the wonderful things God had done in the lives of the Galatians. He had given His Spirit. God had worked miracles. Those things happened in their lives, not because of their law-keeping, but because they had responded in faith to the gospel they had heard.

- *Paul asked the Galatians a question that*
- *showed his astonishment at their deviation*
- *and directed their attention to its unreason-*
- *ableness. "You foolish Galatians! Who has*
- *bewitched you?" Paul followed this dramatic*
- *question with four rhetorical questions to*
- *help the Galatians understand how they had*
- *gone wrong by accepting a false gospel in*
- *place of the true gospel of Jesus Christ.*

THE EXAMPLE OF ABRAHAM (3:6–9)

A Text from Genesis (v. 6)

Paul now turned from experience to Scripture as the basis of his argument. The point he had been making, that salvation comes through faith and not through Law, was proved by Abraham.

"Hearing by Faith"

Much has been written about this expression, which could mean variously "the faculty or organ of hearing," or "the act of hearing." However, while the content of what is heard is crucial, Paul was thinking of the process by which one comes within the orbit of God's saving grace. As Paul said elsewhere, faith comes by hearing and hearing by the Word of God (Rom. 10:17). The term *hearing* refers to the passive posture of the recipient. Thus, Martin Luther could write that the only organs of a Christian are his ears. The focus is not merely on the physical faculty of hearing but on the awakening of faith that comes through the preaching of the gospel. Thus, the contrast Paul was drawing between doing works and believing in Christ.

The patriarch Abraham, who is mentioned nineteen times in Paul's letters, is the pivotal figure in all of Paul's arguments from Scripture in Galatians.

Abraham was the father of the Jewish people, and circumcision began with him (Gen. 17:10–14). But Paul pointed to Gen. 15:6 to show that Abraham's righteousness came as he accepted God's promise by faith. Before Abraham was circumcised, and long before the Law was given to Moses, Abraham was righteous in the sight of God simply by faith in God's promise.

True Children of Abraham (vv. 7–9)

In verse 7 Paul extended his argument from Abraham to his posterity and raised for the first time the question that would dominate the remainder of Galatians 3 and 4: Who are the true children of Abraham? This train of thought later will find a conclusion in the allegory of the two mothers, Sarah and Hagar, and their sons, Isaac and Ishmael (4:21–31).

Abraham was justified not on account of his outstanding virtues and holy works, but solely because he believed God. And his faith was reckoned as righteousness long before he knew anything about circumcision or had taken the first step in his long journey toward the Promised Land. Although he became the father of the Jews, he was justified and he received the Holy Spirit through the hearing of faith, not through works of the Law.

Paul's rebuttal was a stinging rebuke to the theology of the Judaizers. Descent by blood or physical procreation does not create sons of Abraham in the sight of God any more than circumcision does. The true children of Abraham are those who believe—literally, those who ground their very existence on faith in what God has said and done.

In these verses Paul makes two critical points:

1. He redefines the Abrahamic family in such a way as to undercut the appeal of his opponents to this biblical model.

2. Paul interprets the blessing promised through Abraham to "all the nations" as a prophecy of his own law-free mission to the Gentiles.

Paul's entire argument in this passage (vv. 6–9) hinges on one assumption: the continuity of the covenant of grace. From the creation of Adam and Eve until the second coming of Christ, God has provided one and only one way of salvation for all peoples everywhere: The atoning death of His Son on the cross applied to all of the elect through the regenerating ministry of the Holy Spirit.

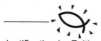

Justification by Faith

Basically, justification is a process by which an individual is brought into an unmerited, right relationship with God. Justification does not encompass the whole salvation process; it does, however, mark that instantaneous point of entry or transformation that makes one "right with God." Christians are justified in the same way Abraham was, by faith (Rom. 4:16; 5:1). Human works do not achieve or earn acceptance by God. The exercise of faith alone ushers us into an unmerited, right relationship with God (Gal. 2:16; Titus 3:7).

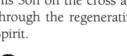

■ *In verses 6–9, Paul turns from his own expe-*
■ *rience to Scripture as the basis of his argu-*
■ *ment. The point he had been making, that*
■ *salvation comes through faith and not*
■ *through Law, was proved by Abraham.*
■ *Abraham was justified not on account of his*
■ *outstanding virtues and holy works, but*
■ *solely because he believed God.*

God speaking to Abram:

"In you all the families of the earth shall be blessed." Gen. 15:3b (NASB)

In verses 6–9 Paul set forth a positive argument for justification by faith. In verses 10–14 he turned the tables and argued negatively against the possibility of justification by works.

CHRIST AND THE CURSE OF THE LAW (3:10–14)

The Curse of the Law (vv. 10–12)

Not only does the Law not bring blessing; it actually imposes a curse. Paul cited Deut. 27:26, which says that anyone who does not keep the Law is cursed. Paul knew that no person could keep all of the Law. Therefore, all were under this curse. Furthermore, Paul maintained that keeping the Law was never intended to be the way to be right with God. Quoting Hab. 2:4, he said, "The righteous will live by *faith*." The original statement in Habakkuk uses *faith* in the sense of faithfulness, but the idea of trusting God is still present.

The way of the Law is different from the way of faith. Quoting Lev. 18:5, Paul pointed out that the Law requires doing, not trusting. The Law dealt with actions. Only if one could do what the Law required could he hope to gain life that way. Thus the Law and the hopeless burden of trying to keep the Law were seen to be a curse.

Redemption through the Cross (vv. 13–14)

Verses 10–12 paint a grim picture of the human situation. The Law requires a life of perfect obedience in order to be right with God. Yet no person can meet such a high standard. Consequently, everyone in the world has become "a prisoner of sin" (3:22), suffering the just condemnation of the curse of the Law. Given this state of affairs, we are prompted to ask with the disciples, "Who then can be saved?" (Luke 18:26).

Paul's answer to this dilemma comes in the form of a confessional statement that may well have circulated in early Jewish Christian communities as a kind of shorthand summary of the gospel itself: Christ "redeemed us from the curse of the law by himself becoming a curse for us." Everything is different for those who trust in Christ. By becoming a curse for us, He has redeemed believers from the curse of the Law.

Paul then quoted Deut. 21:23, which prohibited hanging a body of an executed person from a tree. It was felt that the condemned man was under a curse, and to leave the body publicly displayed would bring a curse on the land. Therefore, the executed person was to be buried and not left in the open. Christ, then, became our substitute and representative, taking upon Himself the curse of the Law.

As an aside, this verse from Deuteronomy may have been a stumbling block to Paul before his encounter with the risen Christ. Knowing this verse and the crucifixion of Jesus, Paul assumed that Jesus was under a curse. For that reason, He couldn't be the Messiah.

Following his conversion, Paul saw that, indeed, Jesus bore a curse but not for Himself. Moreover, the resurrection vindicated Him as God's annointed.

In His death, Jesus broke the curse on humankind and provided the needed alternative. Now in Christ, the blessing God spoke of to Abraham can come to the Gentiles. Anyone who will put his or her faith in Christ can receive the Spirit, the experience of God in his life that comes by being in right relationship with God.

- *One way to summarize this passage is in*
- *terms of two major propositions, each of*

"If a man guilty of a capital offense is put to death and his body is hung on a tree, you must not leave his body on the tree overnight. Be sure to bury him that same day, because anyone hung on a tree is under God's curse. You must not desecrate the land the Lord your God is giving you as an inheritance." Deuteronomy 21:22–23 (NIV)

"Redeemed"

The word *redeemed* means "to buy off" or "set free by the payment of a price." It was used to describe the purchase of slaves. The root word for "*redemption*" is Greek is *agora*, "marketplace," the site of the slave auction where, every day in ancient Rome, human beings were put up for sale to the highest bidder. Paul's use of the word *redemption* declares that we have been bought with a price. The ransom for our sins was nothing less than the life blood of the Son of God.

■ *which is confirmed and clarified by a citation*
■ *from the Old Testament.*

PROPOSITION	OT QUOTE
1. Those who rely on observing the Law are under a curse.	Deut. 27:26
2. No one can be justified by means of the Law.	Hab. 2:4

THE LAW AND THE PROMISED INHERITANCE (3:15–25)

Paul now moves to a second level of argument, where he speaks about the nature of salvation. He shows the validity of the Law as God's free and gracious favor promised to Abraham. This is a favor secured by Christ and sealed in the hearts of believers by the Holy Spirit. Paul argues exclusively from the Scriptures, quoting the Law five times and from the Prophets once. He shows how God's promise to Abraham—that all peoples would be blessed through him—has been fulfilled by Christ, whose death on the cross wrought redemption and justification by faith for Jews and Gentiles alike.

Paul now moves to a second level of argument, showing first how God's covenant with Abraham stands in stark contrast to the Law of Moses and yet how, in the providence of God, even the Law played a crucial role in the unfolding drama of redemption.

The Priority of the Promise (vv. 15–18)

Paul illustrated his argument by giving an example from common experience. He spoke of making a "covenant," likely any kind of contract or formal agreement, such as an exchange of property. His point was that such a contract was binding and was not changed except by the party who made it.

Paul then interrupted his thought to indicate that he was thinking of the covenant God made with Abraham in Genesis 13:15 and 17:7–8.

This covenant was not only promised to Abraham; it was also promised to his offspring (literally "seed"). Paul finds profound significance in the fact that a singular word was used of this offspring. Abraham's seed is Jesus the Messiah, who is head of the new humanity.

Christ was head of the new humanity which God was creating. As such, He included in Himself all who are Abraham's spiritual descendants. Paul is not proving this truth from the Old Testament, simply illustrating from it.

In mentioning the coming of the Law 430 years after Abraham, Paul's point was simply that it was a long time and that the covenant of promise had lasted that long without the addition of the Law. The giving of the Law did not annul God's promise, especially since it was later fulfilled by Christ. If the giving of the Law was intended to provide a new way of receiving God's blessings, then the way of promise would have been anulled.

Covenant

The basic definition of a covenant is a "pact, treaty, alliance, or agreement between two parties of equal or unequal authority." The covenant or testament is a central, unifying theme in Scripture. God made covenants with individuals, and the nation Israel found final fulfillment in the new covenant in Christ Jesus. God's covenants can be understood by humans because they are modeled on human covenants or treaties.

■ *The Law was never intended to replace faith*
■ *in God's promise as the way of salvation.*
■ *There has always been only one way to be*
■ *saved, and it is not by keeping the Law.*

The Purpose of the Law (vv. 19–25)

Structurally, these verses divide neatly into three parts, with the first two sections introduced by leading questions. Paul seems to be speaking in a kind of theological shorthand that is not easy for us to unpack. For this reason, and not ignoring the context of Paul's argument here, we will find that the best commentary on Galatians is the Book of Romans.

Paul's first question is, "What, then, was the purpose of the Law?" This question arises from the logic of Paul's argument that he has pursued relentlessly since 2:16. Paul flings out his answer in four terse statements (vv. 19–20): (1) it was added because of transgressions (cf. Rom. 5:20); (2) until the seed had come, it was put into effect; (3) through angels; (4) by a mediator.

His second question is, "Is the Law, therefore, opposed to the promises of God?" This elicits Paul's immediate and indignant response, "Absolutely not!"

At this point we might think that the Law opposed or contradicted the promise of God. What Paul is saying here is that the Law would be a bad thing if it were given to bring spiritual life and then failed to do so. But no law can bring life. The Law was not given for that purpose, so it cannot be judged a failure on that basis. The Law, like everything else in human experience, was limited by sin.

Paul now moves on to the three functions of the Law.

1. The Law enters that it might fail (v. 21). The failure of the Law to save has been turned into a blessing. The "side road" of

"Absolutely not!"

The Greek expression Paul uses here conveys horror and shock at the very concept under consideration—"absolutely not!" Literally, it can be translated "may it never be!" Or, as A. T. Robertson puts it, "far from it!" Of its fifteen occurrences in the New Testament, thirteen are in Paul's writings. Other occurrences of this expression are in Rom. 3:6, 31; 6:1–2; 9:14; and Gal. 2:17.

the Law, which can only lead to the gallows, has by the great mercy of God directed us back toward the road of salvation.

2. The Law condemns that it might save (vv. 22–23). By exposing human wickedness, the Law eliminates every area of self-justification from which the conscience-driven sinner might draw.

3. The Law disciplines that it might set free (vv. 24–25). The Law is a stern disciplinarian and a harsh taskmaster. Yet in its harshness there is a note of grace, for the function of discipline, as opposed to mere torture, is always remedial. "With its whippings, the Law that draws us to Christ" (Martin Luther, *LW* 26.346).

■ *Because all have sinned, the Law cannot*
■ *bring life. Recognizing this fact leads persons*
■ *to see that only faith in Christ can enable*
■ *them to receive God's promise.*

A Shift in Paul's Argument

The NIV correctly notes a major break in Paul's argument at this point (3:26), a new turn in his continuing scriptural demonstration of the doctrine of justification by faith. To this point Paul has presented the grand sweep of redemptive history from Abraham to Christ. Now he shifts his focus from the historical to the personal, from the institutional to the individual.

The following diagram taken from Timothy George, *Galatians*, New American Commentary, Vol. 30 (Nashville: Broadman & Holman Publishers), page 271.

3:6–14	Promise (Abraham)
	▼
3:15–22	Law (Moses)
	▼
3:23–25	Faith (Christ)
	▼
3:26	"You are all sons of God through faith in Christ Jesus."
	▲
3:27–4:7	Faith (Spirit)
	▲
4:8–11	Law ("the elements of the world")
	▲
4:21–31	Promise (Sarah)

BAPTISM AND THE NEW COMMUNITY (3:26–29)

The New Status of Believers (v. 26)

In this section Paul makes three astounding statements about the new status of "all" true believers.

"To those who believed in his name, he gave the right to become children of God" (John 1:12; cf. Hos. 1:10).

1. "You are all sons of God." Jesus is uniquely and exclusively *the* Son of God, equal with the Father from all eternity, unrivaled by any creatures in His essential deity. All the more remarkable, then, is Paul's description of the redeemed as "sons of God." He developed this theme in the verses that follow by showing how the sonship of Christians derives from the sonship of Christ.

2. "You are all sons of God through faith." Not by natural descent nor human contrivance but through faith alone have we entered into this new relationship with the Heavenly Father.

3. "You are all sons of God through faith in Christ Jesus." The expression "in Christ" is found 172 times in Paul's writings. Most often it is used to describe that participation in and union with Jesus Christ that is effected for every believer by the indwelling of the Holy Spirit.

The Significance of Baptism (vv. 27–29)

For Paul, baptism, with its symbolic association with the death, burial, and resurrection of Christ, models justification, although it can never effect it. For the New Testament believer's baptism with the Holy Spirit is antecedent to baptism with water, the latter being a confession and public witness to the former.

Paul described all that baptism was given to represent in one of the most striking metaphors found anywhere in the New Testament—"putting on" Christ. This comparison could have recalled several parallel practices that would have been familiar to Paul's Gentile converts in Galatia.

"Clothed yourselves with Christ"

In Romans 6–8 Paul connected the concept of putting on Christ with that of "dying and rising with Christ," both of which are dramatically portrayed in the act of baptism. The language of "putting off" and "putting on" is frequently found in Paul's writing, where it often connotes the ethical transformation expected of a true believer.

■ *Paul focuses on the new status the believer*
■ *enjoys through justification by faith. Paul*
■ *then uses the baptismal rite as a symbolic*
■ *model of justification.*

QUESTIONS TO GUIDE YOUR STUDY

1. What is a rhetorical question? How did Paul use this device, and how effective do you think he was in using it to make his point?

Guardianship

The picture in this passage is one of a boy in a home of wealth and standing who is legally the heir. This owner or "young master" of the family estate is still a minor, and so lives under rules very much like a slave.

The guardians Paul refers to may have been the overseers set up by Roman law, a guardian or tutor until age fourteen, and a trustee or curator until age twenty-five. Or the terms may have described a personal guardian and a trustee of property who acted at the same time. These officers acted until the time set by the father. Under Roman law, the father did not set the time for the son to cease being a minor. It is not certain which legal system Paul was thinking about, but there were some parallels in Syrian history.

Paul's point here was that the son, until he became of age, was no better off than a slave. He was under the direction of others.

2. What is the significance of the example of Abraham to Paul's argument on justification by faith?

3. Why is the Law a curse? How is it limiting?

4. According to Paul, what was the purpose of the Law?

GALATIANS 4

THE RADICAL CHANGE: FROM SLAVERY TO SONSHIP (4:1–7)

Our Past Condition (vv. 1–3)

Paul continued to contrast law-keeping and living by faith, presenting another illustration drawn from common experience. He shifts his emphasis from the inheritance to the heir. He describes a child who has been left his father's estate but is too young to take possession of it, and so is placed under guardians and trustees.

We, Paul explained (apparently referring to himself and his readers), were like that. Before the coming of Christ, all were slaves to "the elements of the world."

Two basic interpretations of the phrase "the basic principles of the world" (NIV) are favored:

1. The "basic principles" may be elementary principles, religious and moral "ABCs," such as the Jewish Law.

2. The "basic principles" may be spirits, or spiritual powers, that were thought to move the heavenly bodies.

No matter which interpretation one favors, Paul was speaking of people who lived under the yoke of some force other than the Spirit of God as experienced in Christ.

The Coming of Christ (vv. 4–5)

Verses 4–5 contain one of the most compressed and highly charged passages in the entire letter because they present the objective basis for the doctrine of justification by faith.

Paul and his fellow believers passed out of their immature bondage when Christ came. As in the illustration where the date was set by the father, Christ came "when the time had fully come."

 From the human point of view, Jesus was born at a very favorable time. Roman law, the wonderful system of Roman highways, the political stability maintained by the Romans, the Greek language, and Jewish religious teaching of these all combined to create a situation in which the gospel could spread.

But the emphasis is on God's sovereign choice. God sent His Son into the world. This was a gift of grace. He was born of a woman and shared our human nature. He was born under the Law—that is, He was a Jew and submitted to the curse that the Law imposed. He did this to redeem those who were under the Law.

An examination of the grammatical structure of these verses reveals the four central ideas of the passage brought together within a single literary unit:

1. The *temporal* introduction: "But when the time had fully come."
2. A *parallel participle* describing the condition of the incarnate Son: "Born of a woman."

3. A *parallel participle* describing the status of the incarnate Son: "Born under Law."

4. Two purpose clauses that describe the reason for Christ's coming and the great benefit believers receive through faith in Him: *In order* that He might "redeem those under Law" and *in order* that we might "receive the full rights of sons."

In verse 5 Paul focuses on the divine person and eternal deity of Jesus Christ as it relates to His saving work in redemption and regeneration. The Son of God became a human being and was put under the Law in order to redeem those who were under the Law, and so we might become God's sons.

As redemption implies a basically negative concept—we are redeemed *from* the curse and *from* the slave market of sin—Paul goes on to show the positive purpose for Christ's sacrificial suffering and death. The Son of God was born of woman and put under the Law in order to redeem us from the Law so that we might receive "the full rights of sons."

The Spirit Within (vv. 6–7)

Paul now moves to the Spirit's role as the foundation of our justification by faith. Just as God sent His Son into the world, so He has sent the Spirit of His Son into our hearts.

The best commentary on this text is Paul's parallel statement in Rom. 8:15–16: "For you did not receive a spirit that makes you a slave again to fear, but you received the Spirit of sonship. And by him we cry 'Abba, Father.' The Spirit himself testifies with our spirit that we are God's children." The most basic indication of our adoption is that we have a new form of address for God. The Spirit invites us to join in His invocation, crying, "Abba, Father."

■ *No longer is a person's relationship to God*
■ *determined by race, rank, or role. No longer*
■ *are we under the curse of the Law. The prom-*
■ *ise given to Abraham and fulfilled in his pro-*
■ *phetic Seed, Jesus Christ, has now been*
■ *extended to all of those who through faith in*
■ *Him have become sons, crying "Abba!" and*
■ *heirs of the living God.*

AREA OF THEOLOGY	KEY DOCTRINE	GALATIANS PASSAGE
Study of Christ	Our adoption as sons	4:4
Study of Salvation	Our redemption through the cross	4:5
Study of the Spirit	Our regeneration through the Spirit	4:6–7

Abba

Abba is the Aramaic word for "father." It is the term a child would have used much as children today use "Daddy." It is still heard throughout the Middle East as a word of address used by young children to greet their father. However, Abba, used here in Galatians, is more associated with intimacy than infancy. Jesus introduced its use in reference to God. Before that, it would have been considered much too familiar and personal. Those who are in Christ enter into this intimate relation with God and inherit the promises of God.

From 3:6 through 4:7, Paul develops a tightly woven and carefully crafted argument for the doctrine of justification by faith. He offers an analysis of redemptive history centered on the true identity of the children of Abraham. The remainder of chapter 4 can be divided into three literary units:

Verses 8–11 are an exhortation in which Paul reminds his Galatian converts of their former way of life, the great transformation that has happened to them through their adoption into

God's family, and his deep concern that they are about to exchange their spiritual heritage for a "mess of pottage."

Verses 12–20 extend the theme of Paul's fear by his recalling the endearing bonds of friendship and love he and the Galatians had enjoyed in days past. He pleads with them to remain faithful to the one and only gospel he had first preached among them.

Verses 21–31 contain the allegory of Hagar and Sarah whose sons, Ishmael and Isaac, are taken as representative types of spiritual slavery and spiritual sonship.

"Turning Back"

Some have implied that by using the phrase "turning back," Paul was implying that the Galatians could lose their salvation. It is significant that the word Paul uses for "turning back" is a technical term used for both religious conversion (1 Thess. 1:9; Acts 9:35; 15:19) and religious apostasy (2 Pet. 2:21–22). However, real apostasy, as opposed to a temporary backsliding, is possible only for those who have never been genuinely converted.

THE DANGER OF TURNING BACK (4:8–11)

Before the Galatians became Christians, they worshiped the pagan deities. Paul acknowledged their existence as some kind of spirits, but he denied that they were gods. Those who worshiped them were in bondage to them. Then the Galatians came to know God, or as Paul put it, "to be known by God." This emphasizes the fact that God takes the initiative. Our relationship with Him does not depend on our intiative.

To turn to the works of the Law would be to give up this relationship and return to a state of bondage. Paul implies that bondage to the Law is the same as their bondage to pagan gods. Both systems demanded that their followers observe special days and seasons. Both systems were heavily motivated by fear and kept their adherents uncertain and intimidated.

This would have been one of the appeals that Jewish legalism made to former pagans. Both the works of the Law and the pagan gods were "weak and miserable principles [spirits]." Both lacked power to save and to bring abundant life.

The thought of the Galatians accepting such a condition made Paul feel that he had failed. We can understand Paul's feeling here, as it is possible that some may have "tasted the goodness of the word of God and the powers of the coming age" (Heb. 6:5) without being converted. This helps us make sense of his closing lamentation, "I fear for you, that somehow I have wasted my efforts on you."

- *To turn to the works of the Law would be to give up a relationship with God and "knowing Him" to return to a state of bondage. Paul rebuked the Galatian believers to keep them from being drawn into a legalistic religious system.*

PAUL'S PERSONAL APPEAL (4:12–20)

This section forms a personal parenthesis in Paul's overall argument for justification by faith, which he resumes and concludes in verses 21–31 with an additional proof from Scripture.

Paul's Labors among the Galatians (vv. 12–16)

The mention of his work previously among the Galatians led Paul to speak very personally of his ministry in Galatia. He began with a strong appeal for the Galatians to "become like me"—that is, free from the Law. This he urged "for I became like you." Becoming like them may mean that Paul had virtually become a Gentile. Or perhaps it referred to the fact that he had once been in bondage to the Law and had

Paul's Affliction

Verse 13 has fascinated scholars primarily because of its reference to the undisclosed illness which afflicted Paul during his first visit to Galatia. In the early church, Jerome interpreted Paul's affliction as the temptation of sexual desire that he identified with the "thorn in the flesh" of 2 Cor. 12:7. During the Reformation, Martin Luther dismissed a reference to the suffering and affliction Paul bore as the result of the persecutions he endured.

In recent years, however, most commentators have discarded both of those traditional interpretations in favor of the idea that Paul was referring here in Galatians to some actual bodily illness that affected his missionary labors.

been set free. In either case, Paul was telling his readers that he had a lot in common with them. He knew what they were going through and urged them to follow his example.

 Paul was a pioneer in what we call today *contextualization*, the communication of the gospel in such a way that it speaks to the total context of the people to whom it is addressed. Insofar as we are able to separate the heart of the gospel from its cultural cocoon—to contextualize the message of Christ without compromising its content—we too should become imitators of Paul.

Paul's Love for Them (vv. 17–20)

Before declaring again (vv. 19–20) his enduring love and anguished concern for the Galatians, Paul took a long sidewards glance at his opponents, whose evil activities had precipitated the present crisis in Paul's relationship with the Galatians. Neither here nor anywhere else in Galatians did Paul name these troublesome agitators. The problem with the agitators was not the interest they had shown in the Galatians, but their evil intentions and selfish motivation ("it is for their own ends," Phillips; "but for a dishonorable purpose," Knox).

In the midst of his argument for justification by faith, Paul made a personal appeal to the Galatians. He appealed to them to "become like me"—that is, free from the Law. Paul told his readers that he had a lot in common with them, he knew what they were going through, and he urged them to follow his example.

THE ANALOGY OF HAGAR AND SARAH (4:21–31)

The Analogy (vv. 21–23)

Paul now brings his doctrinal argument to a climax. He calls for the attention of those who were considering putting themselves under the Law and asks whether they had really heard what the Law said. After all, Paul was a lifelong student of the Law and trained in the schools of the rabbis. He proceeds to pick up again the theme of Abraham and his descendants by pointing to the story of Abraham, Sarah, and Hagar.

Hagar, the slave woman, symbolized Mount Sinai, the system of obedience to the Mosaic Law. Her son Ishmael represented those enslaved to legalism. Sarah corresponded to the freedom in Christ. Her son Isaac represented spiritual children of Abraham, who were freed from the Law by faith in Christ. The Galatians were the children born in freedom, but they acted as if they were the descendants of the slave-wife. Paul urged them to take their stand in freedom to avoid the harness of slavery (5:1).

The Figurative Meaning (vv. 24–27)

In verse 24 we come to one the most difficult and controversial words in the entire epistle. Referring to the historical summary he had just given in verses 22–23, Paul declared, "These things may be taken figuratively." Allegorical interpretation seeks to discern a hidden meaning in a given story or text—a meaning that may be divorced from the historical events and facts alluded to in the text itself.

Typology

A method of interpretation wherby Christian truths are symbolized in Old Testament events.

Clearly, however, Paul was not advocating a departure from the basic meaning of Scripture as found in its natural and literal sense. What he called an allegory might be better termed *typology*: a narrative from Old Testament history interpreted in terms of new covenant realities.

The entire analogy involves five sets of twos: two mothers, two sons, two covenants, two mountains (Mount Sinai and Mount Zion, the latter being understood, but not expressed), and two cities. The following chart contrasts the two women and what they represent.

HAGAR	SARAH
Ishmael, the son of slavery	Isaac, the son of freedom
Birth "according to the flesh"	Birth "through the promise"
Old Covenant	New Covenant
Mount Sinai	Mount Zion
Present Jerusalem	Heavenly Jerusalem

The two women stood for two covenants—law and promise. The law covenant, represented by Hagar, came from Mount Sinai. This was where Moses received the Law. It was not located in the Promised Land but in Arabia, the area settled by the descendants of Ishmael. Paul links Hagar and Jerusalem, the center of Judaism and the Law. She and her children were slaves. It must have come as a shock to the Judaizers to read this, for the Jews would have said they descended from Isaac, not Ishmael. They thought they were free, not slaves, as they said to Jesus on one occasion (John 8:33).

However, Paul was speaking not of biological relationships but spiritual realities. The Judaizers insisted on the slavery of the Law, and the Isaac family was characterized by freedom and promise.

Sarah represented the Jerusalem above, a New Testament designation of the church and the heavenly home of God's people (Heb. 12:22; Rev. 3:12; 21:2, 9ff). This Jerusalem is free and is the mother of all who are in Christ.

Paul breaks into a joyful quotation from Isa. 54:1, in which the fruitfulness of restored Jerusalem is contrasted with the barrenness of Jerusalem destroyed by the conquerors. Sarah had been barren, and the church might seem barren at times. But according to God's promise, the children of freedom would be many. Paul reminded the Galatians that they, along with him, belonged in the Isaac family, the family of promise.

"the Lord says, 'Sing, Jerusalem.

You are like a woman who never gave birth to children

Start singing and shout for joy.

You never felt the pain of giving birth, but you will have more children than the woman who has had a husband.'"
Isa. 54:1 (NCV)

■ *Paul brings his doctrinal argument to a cli-*
■ *max by pointing to the story of Abraham,*
■ *Sarah, and Hagar. He uses typology, a nar-*
■ *rative from Old Testament history that he*
■ *interprets in terms of new covenant realities.*
■ *With this analogy, Paul makes his point that*
■ *the Galatians, along with him, belonged to*
■ *the family of promise.*

THE PERSONAL APPLICATION (4:28–31)

 Quoting from Gen. 21:8–14, Paul adapts the words of Sarah concerning Ishmael to the situation in Galatia: "Cast out the slave woman and her son!" This passage from Genesis speaks of Sarah's displeasure at the continued presence of Ishmael alongside Isaac. Later Jewish tradition spoke of the persecution of Isaac by Ishmael.

Paul sees a reenactment of this in the trouble being given the Galatians by the Judaizers.

Sarah had demanded that Hagar and Ishmael be sent away. The inheritance could not go to both the slave's son and the free woman's son. Paul is calling for a strong solution to the problem in Galatia. The legalists would have to be cast out. He again reminds the Galatians in verse 31 that they were the children of freedom.

QUESTIONS TO GUIDE YOUR STUDY

1. Describe the doctrine of adoption. What does it include?
2. Why was the concept of sonship such good news for those who were in bondage to the Law?
3. What danger did Paul warn the Galatians about? What stake did he have in their growth as believers?
4. What is the significance of Paul's analogy of Hagar and Sarah?

GALATIANS 5

SECTION INTRODUCTION: THE PRACTICAL ARGUMENT (5:2–6:10)

Chapter 5 begins Paul's practical, concluding section. In this final section Paul warned against the cavalier attitude that freedom from the Law created in some people who lived in disobedience. He reminded the Galatians that they must respond to the urgings of the Holy Spirit and not be captured by the cravings of the flesh. He also entreated them to show concern for one another and to demonstrate persistence in their commitment to Christ.

A PASSIONATE CALL TO FREEDOM IN CHRIST (5:1–12)

Stand Firm in Freedom (v. 1)

Verse 1 is a transitional sentence and could easily be connected with chapter 4. It is a stirring challenge to embrace freedom, not slavery. If Galatians is the Magna Carta of Christian liberty, then Gal. 5:1 has reason to be considered one of the key verses of the epistle.

Falling from Grace (vv. 2–6)

Verses 2–3 state two terrible consequences of a lapse into legalism for the Galatians: (1) it would cancel the benefits of Christ for them, and (2) it would put them under the necessity of keeping all of the Law. Perhaps the Galatians had not thought of it, but they could not submit to circumcision and stop there. Once they had admitted that this was necessary, they would be admitting that all the rest of the Law was necessary. As James noted, to break one point of the Law was to be guilty of all the Law (Jas. 2:10).

"Remember that a man who keeps the whole Law but fr a single exception is none the less a law breaker."
James 2:10, (Phillips)

Paul spoke further on the first danger, the result of turning to the Law, which cancels the benefits of Christ in a person's life. Paul explained that for those who turn to the Law, "Christ will be of no value" to them. That is because the way of Christ is a totally different approach to righteousness. If Christ and the Law were simply two items in a category of ways to please God, then by all means they should have used both. But the way of the Law is the way of human effort, and the way of Christ is denial of human effort. The two are mutually exclusive.

"Whoever wants to have a half-Christ loses the whole."

—John Calvin
[Taken from Calvin, CNTC 11.93.]

Paul carries the idea further in verse 4 where he says, "You who are trying to be justified by Law have been alienated from Christ; you have fallen away from grace." Such a person removes himself or herself from the relationship in which Christ can be of benefit. Such a person has "fallen away from grace."

Because that phrase has come to mean to some that a person may be saved through faith in Christ and later lose his or her salvation through some sin that they commit, it requires careful study. We need to note first that Paul is speaking of the catastrophic loss of the benefits of Christ. This clear statement should not be explained away. (It has been suggested, for example, that they would have been fallen from sanctifying grace, but not from justifying grace.) But it is equally clear that Paul is not speaking of losing salvation by committing sin. He is speaking of substituting Law for grace as the basis of salvation.

Second, we must remember that Paul is talking about a hypothetical situation. For emphasis he is speaking as if the Galatians had already fallen from grace. He is simply carrying his argument to its logical conclusion to show the Galatians how great their danger. His concern here is practical guidance, not theoretical argument.

The promise of righteousness through the Law is appealing because it is definite and tangible. The righteousness that comes through faith, Paul argues, is no less real. Although this righteousness may not be fully experienced until God's final judgment, it is already present in the form of hope as the Spirit works in the believer now.

Verse 6 is a key as it cuts through all the debate about circumcision to show what really matters. Circumcision accomplished nothing, but neither did uncircumcision. It was an equally serious error if the Galatians refused circumcision and then prided themselves on that, thinking they had earned some merit in the sight of God. There can be a legalism of doing and a legalism of not doing. The only thing that really matters is "faith expressing itself through love."

Circumcision or the Cross (vv. 7–12)

"Who cut in on you?" is a rhetorical question similar to "Who has bewitched you?" in 3:1. The result in this sinister interference in the life race of the Galatians is that they had not continued to obey the truth. Earlier in his letter, Paul had summarized his entire message under the rubric the "truth of the gospel" (2:5, 14). This was precisely what the Galatians were on the verge of deserting through their alliance with the unbelieving theology of false teachers. Here Paul is calling them back from the brink of disaster.

 We find three important applications in verse 7:

1. The Christian life is a marathon, not a hundred-yard dash. Paul wanted the Galatians who began so well to finish well also. Ministers have a special responsibility to disciple and nurture young believers so they may stay the course and not be deterred by the hinderers who will surely come.

2. Paul did not give up on the Galatians even though many of them had shifted their loyalty from him to the usurpers and, to all outward appearances, appeared to be lost for the cause of God and truth. From God's perspective, of course, no person who has been genuinely regenerated will ever utterly or finally fall away from the faith (John 10:28; Rom. 8:29; Eph. 1:4–6).

"Running a Race"

Paul compares the Christian life to the running of a race, an athletic image found in many of his writings (1 Cor. 9:24–26; Phil. 3:14; 2 Tim 4:7). The image is of an Olympic athlete who dashes from the starting line with great vigor, perhaps accelerating past his competitors, only to have someone from the stands suddenly enter the race and trip him at an unexpected turn in the road.

Paul had "confidence" that the Galatians could be won back and thus labored strenuously to that end. So must every minister of the gospel who counsels with those who may be tempted to abandon the race they have begun.

3. The "truth of the gospel" is not only something to be believed but also something to be obeyed. Having forsaken the solid theological foundation Paul laid for them, the Galatians soon found themselves awash in immorality and debauchery of all kinds. By undermining their confidence in sound doctrine, Satan seduced them into loose living. Nowhere do we see more clearly the correlation between doctrinal integrity and spiritual vitality.

As Paul continues his letter, he speaks of the methods of the false teachers and considers the end result of their meddlesome interference. He does this by quoting a proverbial saying from the world of breadmaking: "It takes only a little yeast to make the whole batch of dough rise" (TEV). This is a commonsense saying similar to our own English maxim, "Just one rotten apple spoils the whole barrel."

Paul's point is clear: His opponents had not overturned the whole system of Christian teaching but were only making a seemingly minor adjustment to it—the imposition of the harmless rite of circumcision. But even a seemingly slight deviation on such a fundamental matter of the faith can bring total ruin to the Christian community. Just a little poison, if it is toxic enough, will destroy the entire body.

Verse 9 ended on a note of sourdough, a batch of bread thoroughly infested from a little morsel of yeast. The churches in Galatia were in turmoil. They were wavering and perhaps even tilting toward Paul's opponents, but they had not yet completely succumbed to the false teachers' persuasive appeals. Paul's primary purpose in writing his letter probably was to provide a counterweight to the false teachers.

Evidently a part of the "confusion" in verse 10 stemmed from a false accusation, a slanderous lie, that Paul's opponents had circulated about him when they first came into contact with the Galatians. In urging circumcision upon the Gentile believers there, they apparently whispered, "Haven't you heard that Paul himself is an advocate of circumcision?" To us this seems like a preposterous charge, and Paul certainly thought it to be maliciously intended.

Verse 12 is the strongest statement in the epistle, and it showed how deeply disturbed Paul was over this crisis. It has been considered by some as the most startling of all Paul's recorded statements in the New Testament. In referring to the act of circumcision, Paul expresses his wish that those preaching circumcision "would go the whole way and emasculate themselves." The Jerusalem Bible translates verse 12, "Tell those who are disturbing you I would like to see the knife slip." However we choose to translate verse 12, we must not imagine that Paul meant any literal, physical harm to his opponents. He did not fight with carnal weapons but rather with "the sword of the Spirit, which is the word of God" (Eph. 6:17).

"Persuasion"

It is obvious that the circumcision-preaching agitators had exerted a powerful influence over Paul's converts. They had bewitched them and tripped them up in their race toward the finish line. What was the secret of their success? Paul answered this question by using (v. 8) a unique word, "the persuasion" (Gr. *peismone*), a term found nowhere else in earlier Greek literature.

■ *In this section, Paul describes the dangers of*
■ *giving in to the Judaizers' demand for cir-*
■ *cumcision. We feel the clash of turbulent and*
■ *conflicting emotions as Paul vacillates*
■ *between consolation and anger, exasperation*
■ *and hope. Paul registered many strong words*
■ *against the Judaizers whose false teachings*
  were poisoning the Galatian churches.

FLESH AND THE SPIRIT (5:13–26)

The Law of Love (vv. 13–15)

"The only bondage in God's Creation that is tolerable and desirable is the law of love. No man knows true happiness till he has learned how to love—how to love not a little, but a great deal."

Henry Ward Beecher, "The Fruits of the Spirit" from *20 Centuries of Great Preaching*, vol. IV, p. 316 (Waco: Word Books, 1971).

Paul once again repeats his challenge. As in verse 1, he points to freedom. As in verse 8 he reminds them of his calling. As he had done several times before (3:15; 4:12, 31), he calls them brothers. Then, having made his point about freedom, he clarifies what that Christian freedom means. There is always the danger that freedom will be mistaken for license. It could become, Paul said, "an occasion to the flesh." By "flesh," Paul meant human nature without the motivation of the Holy Spirit.

If the Christian is not under the Law, then what is to prevent him from giving in to the desires of the flesh? Paul's answer to this question is, the commitment to be servants of one another through love! This is what the Law is all about. If you love your neighbor as yourself (Lev. 19:18; Luke 10:27), then you have fulfilled the intent of the Law (Rom. 13:8–10). Thus Paul showed that he did not deny what the Law aimed at, which was righteousness. He simply said that the Law cannot bring it about; but Christ can.

Life without love would be chaos and destruction. This is true of legalism as well as license. Without love, persons would "keep on biting and devouring each other" like wild animals tearing at each other's throats.

Conflict and Victory (vv. 16–18)

Paul has just described the kind of life that lapses into uncontrolled indulgences of the flesh. He now presents the Christian alternative, which is not law but the Spirit. Paul uses several distinct verbs to illustrate the Spirit-controlled life of the believer, all of which are roughly equivalent in meaning. He urges believers to:

1. Be led by the Spirit (v. 18).
2. Live by the Spirit (v. 25a).
3. Keep in step with the Spirit (v. 25b).

Each of these verbs suggests a relationship of dynamic interaction, direction, and purpose. The Spirit in the life of the believer means the presence and power of God in the believer's life.

PICTURES OF *FLESH* IN THE NEW TESTAMENT

The fifteen items Paul lists in his "catalog of evil" are by no means intended to be exhaustive. And so as he concludes his list, he adds "and the like."

Sins of Immorality:

Sexual Immorality. It is significant that the first three acts in Paul's list of sins have to do with loose sexual relations. This typically Pauline feature characterizes his listing of evil offenses in other writings as well (1 Cor. 6:9; 6:18; Eph. 5:5; 1 Thess. 4:3).

The Greek word for "sexual immorality" originally meant "prostitution." By Paul's time, it was used to denote a whole range of immoral sexual

Flesh

The word *flesh* as translated by the KJV (Gr. *sarx*) is a complex term with various meanings, depending on the context in which it is used. Elsewhere in Galatians Paul uses the word *flesh* to refer to human life in its material dimension, our physical body, or to that which is merely human as opposed to spiritual or divine (2:20; 4:29, KJV). However, throughout Gal. 5–6, flesh is used as an ethical term with a decidedly negative connotation. Flesh refers to fallen human nature, the center of human pride. Flesh is the arena of indulgence and self-assertion. We cannot restrict the use of the term *flesh* to the human body, although the "works of the flesh" Paul will shortly describe (5:19–21, KJV) are manifested in connection with bodily life. Paul warns the Galatians that they must not turn their freedom into license or use it as an occasion to gratify their fleshly desires.

relationships, including incest (1 Cor. 5:1). For believers to be caught up in sexual misconduct deeply grieves the Holy Spirit, whose presence within their lives has made of their bodies temples unto the Lord.

Acts of sexual immorality, although often done in the name of love, are really the antithesis of love, which is the foremost fruit of the Spirit.

Impurity. This word literally means "uncleanness" and has both a medical and ceremonial connotation. Even today doctors speak of cleaning a wound before they apply medication to it.

Under the Mosaic Law, ceremonial impurity barred one from participation in the worship rituals of the temple until the impediment was removed. Uncleanness, then, speaks of the defilement of sexual sin and the separation from God that it brings. The remedy for such sins is confession and repentance. If we confess and repent, the promise of God's Word is that Christ is faithful and just to forgive and purify us from all unrighteousness (1 John 1:9).

Debauchery. William Barclay defines this particular vice as "a love of sin so reckless and so audacious that a man has ceased to care what God or man thinks of his actions" (*Flesh and Spirit: An Examination of Galatians 5:19–23* (London: SCM, 1962), 31). Debauchery speaks of the total loss of limits, the lack of restraint, decency, and self-respect.

Sins of Idolatry:

Idolatry. From the ancient fertility cult of Baal to the sacral prostitution at the temple of Aphrodite in Corinth, the homage paid to false gods was often accompanied by shameful displays of sensuality. It is significant that the word *idolatry* is not found in the texts of the classical writers but belongs to the unique Christian vocabulary of the New Testament.

Witchcraft. At the root of this word is *pharmakon*, literally "drug." In classical Greek, the word *pharmakeia* referred to the use of drugs, whether for medicinal or more sinister purposes (e.g., poisoning). In the New Testament, however, it is invariably associated with the occult, both here in Galatians and in Revelation, where it occurs twice (Rev. 9:21; 18:23).

Sins of Animosity:

Hatred. This is the first of eight nouns Paul mentions, all of which refer to the breakdown of interpersonal relationships. Hatred or enmity (cf. "quarrels," NEB) is the opposite of love. In Rom. 8:7 Paul used the same word to describe the hostility of the sinful mind to God. Here in Galatians, however, its destructive force is played out on the plane of human relationships. The specific forms this hatred can take in tearing down community life are: discord, jealousy, fits of rage, selfish ambition, dissensions, factions, envy.

Discord. In the New Testament this word is unique to Paul, who used it nine times to characterize the strife and discord that beset so many of his congregations. Paul was aware of some who even preached Christ "out of envy and rivalry" (Phil. 1:15). This shows that it is possible for the servants of the Lord to use even unworthy motives and selfish means to accomplish the greatest good. But the damage is done to the body of Christ when ministers of the gospel do not walk in the Spirit, but are pulled aside by petty bickering and pride!

In New Testament times, drugs were used for occult purposes including, and especially, abortion. In the early church both infanticide, often effected through the exposure of newborn babies to the harsh elements; and abortion, commonly brought about by the use of drugs; were regarded as murderous acts. Both are flagrant violations of Jesus' command to "love your neighbor as yourself."

Jealousy often leads to bitterness and sometimes erupts into violence, as when Joseph's brothers seized him in anger and sold him into slavery (Gen. 37:12–26). At the root of all sentiments of jealousy is the basic posture of ingratitude to God, a failure to accept one's life as a gift from God. To envy what someone else has is to fling one's own gifts before God in rebellion and spite.

Jealousy. Jealousy can be used in the Bible in a good sense to describe even God Himself. But here, Paul uses the word with a negative connotation. A jealous person is someone who wants what other people have. A jealous pastor looks with envious eyes on the more prosperous church field of a neighboring minister.

Fits of Rage. Here is another word (one word in the Greek New Testament) with various shades of meaning, depending on the context in which it is used. For example, this same word is used in Revelation to refer both to God's wrath (14:10; 19:15) and Satan's rage (12:12). Here in Galatians it means a passionate outburst of anger or hostile feeling.

Such displays of uncontrollable verbal violence should not be excused as the product of "an Irish temper" or a natural propensity to "fly off the handle." Such fits of rage are a form of conduct unbecoming to a Christian. They drag us away from God and the promptings of His Spirit and further enmesh us in the works of the flesh.

Selfish Ambition. This is a term that derives from the political culture of ancient Greece, where it meant "office seeking" or "canvassing for office." Although many godly men and women have been called to live out their Christian vocation in political life, it is also true that politics attracts those persons given to self-promotion and self-service rather than the service of others. For such "political animals," climbing the ladder of success or manipulating the process for personal gain is all a part of a self-seeking lifestyle.

While the characteristics are bad enough in secular politics, they are especially corrupting to the community of faith whose Lord and Savior modeled the opposite of this vice. He came not to be served but to serve—to give His life as a ransom for many.

Dissensions. Paul used this word only on one other occasion (Rom. 16:17). "Dissensions" carries political overtones suggesting the cultivation of a party spirit or exclusive elite within the church. Whenever this happens, the unity and fellowship of the body of Christ fractures. Soon the backbiting, badmouthing, and mutual destruction Paul warned the Galatians of (5:15) manifest themselves to the detriment of the life and witness of God's people.

Factions. This word also occurs only one other time in Paul's writings. In 1 Cor. 11:19 Paul speaks of the various factions in the church at Corinth. The basic meaning of the word *factions* comes from the verb "to choose" (from which we also get our English word *heresy*). This verse from 1 Corinthians reminds us that the divisive tendency so evident in many congregations is the result of intentional choices to walk in the way of selfish pride, envy, and bickering rather than the royal road of love, forgiveness, and magnanimity.

The English word *heresy* is a derivative of the Greek word translated here as "factions."

Envy. This is another word similar in meaning to the trait of jealousy listed earlier, except that this word is plural, suggesting the multitudinous expressions of envious desire. Here in Gal. 5:21 it refers to the unacceptable rivalry that had sprung up from the malice and ill will of the Galatians toward one another.

Sins of Intemperance:

Drunkenness. We come now to the fourth group of sinful deeds Paul included in his catalog of the works of the flesh. There is no place for drunkenness in a Spirit-directed life. Alcohol abuse was a common feature of urban life in the

Roman Empire, but Paul expected a higher standard of conduct among those who belonged to Christ.

He later wrote to the Ephesians: "Do not get drunk on wine, which leads to debauchery. Instead, be filled with the Spirit" (Eph. 5:18). In addition to the common abuse of alcohol, Paul may also have had in mind the cultic inebriation practiced by the mystery religion of Dionysos, the wine god. Some of those who were in the habit of getting drunk before participating in the Lord's Supper at Corinth may have been influenced by this pagan ritual (1 Cor. 11:21). Paul portrayed excessive drinking as incompatible with real Christian commitment.

Orgies. This word is variously translated "revelings" (KJV), "carousing" (NRSV), "wild parties" (TLB). It occurs three times in the New Testament (here and in Rom. 13:13 and 1 Pet. 4:3). In each case it is linked to the sin of drunkenness. In New Testament times, as in our day, the abuse of alcohol contributed to marital infidelity, child and spouse abuse, the erosion of family life, and the moral chaos in society.

■ *Throughout Gal. 5:19–21, Paul leads us*
■ *down fifteen steps into the pit of depravity.*
■ *He shows us the ugly reality of the flesh. He*
■ *could have gone on and on as he indicates by*
■ *his closing tag "and the like." Only divine*
■ *grace, through the transforming power of the*
■ *Spirit, can rescue us from the snare of such a*
■ *loveless life.*

A Catalog of Evil

SINS OF IMMORALITY	SINS OF IDOLATRY	SINS OF ANIMOSITY:	SINS OF INTEMPERANCE:
Sexual immorality	Idolatry	Hatred	Drunkenness
Impurity	Witchcraft	Discord	Orgies
Debauchery		Jealousy	
		Fits of rage	
		Selfish ambition	
		Dissensions	
		Factions	
		Envy	

The Fruit of the Spirit (vv. 22–26)

After listing fifteen specific misdeeds—fifteen one-word illustrations of the works of the flesh—Paul turns to consider the contrasting graces of the Spirit-controlled life.

Paul groups these nine graces into three triads that give a sense of order and completion, although there is no attempt to provide an exhaustive list of the Christian virtues.

Love. The word is used frequently by Paul. It is significant that love heads the list of these nine graces of the Christian life. Paul might well have placed a period after love and moved on to the conclusion of his letter.

Love is not merely "first among equals" in this listing, but rather the source and fountain from which all of the other graces flow. Love as a characteristic of the Christian life issues from God's unfathomable love and infinite mercy toward us.

It is supremely important that Christians learn to live together in love. When Christians forget this, two horrible consequences follow. First, the worship of

For Paul, love was foundational to everything he had and would yet say in Galatians—"I live by faith in the Son of God, who loved me and gave himself for me" (Gal. 2:20). The result of the transforming, sanctifying ministry of the Holy Spirit in our lives is just this: We are enabled to love one another with the same kind of love that God loves us. Paul profiled this kind of love in 1 Corinthians 13.

the church is disrupted as the gifts of the Spirit are placed in competition with the fruit of the Spirit, as happened in Corinth. Second, the witness of the church is damaged as unbelievers stumble and fall over the obvious lack of love within the body of Christ.

Christian joy is marked by celebration and expectation of God's ultimate victory over the powers of sin and darkness—a victory actualized already in the death and resurrection of Jesus Christ, who "for the joy set before him endured the cross" (Heb. 12:2), but now has been exalted at the right hand of the Father from where He will come in power and glory.

 Joy. Paul repeatedly emphasized the divine origin of joy, encouraging believers to rejoice "in the Lord" (Phil. 3:1; 4:4), "rejoice in God" (Rom. 5:11). The Greek root for *joy* is the same as that for *grace.* Obviously, there is a close connection between the two concepts. Joy is also closely related to *hope*, a word Paul did not list in his catalog of the Spirit's fruit.

 Peace. Just as true joy cannot be gauged by the absence of unpleasant circumstances, so neither can peace be defined in terms of the cessation of violence, war, and strife. The Hebrew concept of peace is much more positive than that, referring to a condition of wholeness and well-being that includes both a right relationship with God and loving harmony with one's fellow human beings. Paul speaks both of "peace with God," the consequence of being justified by faith, and the "peace of God," which transcends human understanding (Rom. 5:1; Phil. 4:7).

"The fabric is built up, story by story. Love is the foundation, joy the superstructure, peace the crown of all."

—J. B. Lightfoot [Taken from J. B. Lightfoot, *Galatians*, 212.]

The triad love-joy-peace was a familiar watchword among the early Christians, and comparable to faith, hope, and love. Clearly these three graces cover the whole range of Christian existence.

Patience. Patience refers to that quality of mind that takes everything in stride and is not easily offended. It is the ability to put up with other people even when that is not an easy thing to do. Patience in this sense, of course, is preeminently a characteristic of God. If God is long-suffering with us, should we not display this same grace in our relationships with one another? This quality should characterize the life of every believer, but it has a special relevance for those who are called to teach and preach the Word of God (2 Tim. 4:2).

John Chrysostom, bishop of Constantinople, defined *patience* as a spirit which could take revenge but chooses not to.

Kindness. Like patience, kindness is a characteristic of God intended to be reproduced by the Spirit in God's people. God is forbearing and kind toward sinners in His wooing of them to salvation (Rom. 2:4). Kindness is not sentimentality, and Paul admonished believers to observe both "the kindness and the sternness of God" (Rom. 11:22). Paul frequently appeals to Christians to "be kind to one another" and to clothe themselves with kindness (Eph. 4:32; Col. 3:12). Where was this Christian grace to be seen among the Galatians who were biting, devouring, and consuming one another?

Goodness. This is a rare word found only four times in the New Testament (and only in Paul). It conveys the idea of benevolence and generosity toward someone else—going the second mile when it is not required. We sometimes speak of a deed done "out of the goodness of one's heart," which comes close to the meaning here except that, as with all nine items in the list, we are dealing with ethical characteristics produced in the believer by the Holy Spirit—not with natural qualities or personality traits cultivated apart from this supernatural dynamic.

Faithfulness. The word *faith* bears several distinct meanings in the New Testament, three of which are represented in Galatians. First, there is faith in the sense of the basic content of the Christian message, *the* faith once delivered to the saints. Paul uses the word *faith* in this sense in Gal. 1:2, where he speaks of the report that circulated about him following his dramatic conversion: "The man who formerly persecuted us is now preaching *the* faith he once tried to destroy." More commonly, *faith* refers to one's acceptance.

As an expression of the fruit of the Spirit, gentleness is strength under control, power harnessed in loving service and respectful actions. One who is gentle in this sense will not attempt to push others around or arrogantly impose one's own will on subordinates or peers.

Gentleness. This word connotes a submissive and teachable spirit toward God that manifests itself in genuine humility and consideration toward others. It is regrettable that the English word *gentleness* has come to have the popular connotation of a wimpish weakness and nonassertive lack of vigor.

Gentleness is not incompatible with decisive action and firm convictions. It was, after all, Jesus who expelled the mercenaries from the temple because of their defilement of His Father's house. This same Jesus is meek and humble (Matt. 11:29).

 Self-Control. This word refers to the mastery over one's desires and passions. In 1 Cor. 7:9, Paul uses this expression in a context related to the control of sexual impulses and desires. That idea is certainly included here in Galatians as well, although self-control as a Christian virtue cannot be restricted to matters of sexuality. Paul's athletic imagery for the Christian life helps us interpret this word.

That self-control appears last in Paul's list may indicate its importance as a summation of the preceding virtues. It would have been particularly relevant for the Galatians setting: antinomians veering out of control reinforced by a new respect for God's moral law.

In 1 Cor. 9:24–27 Paul compared Christians to athletes who must undergo strict training in order to compete as a runner or boxer. A Christian without self-control is like a racer who runs aimlessly from one side of the course to the other or a boxer who pummels the air, never landing a blow.

■ *After cataloging fifteen sins that are the*
■ *works of the flesh, Paul contrasts them with*
■ *the fruit of the Spirit. These three triads of*
■ *the Christian graces are evidences of a*
■ *Spirit-filled life.*

A CATALOG OF GRACE

Love
Joy
Peace
Patience
Kindness
Goodness
Faithfulness
Gentleness
Self-Control

QUESTIONS TO GUIDE YOUR STUDY

1. What are the critical contrasts between the works of the flesh and the fruit of the Spirit?
2. What did Paul mean when he cautioned the Galatians not to "fall from grace"?
3. Paul labels the nine Christian virtues which he describes as the "fruit of the Spirit." What are the implications of the term *fruit*?
4. How might we go about cultivating the fruit of the Spirit in our lives?

FREEDOM IN SERVICE TO OTHERS (6:1–10)

Thus far in his exhortation, Paul has presented the case for Christian ethics—not in terms of a general theory of human behavior, but as the unfolding of the principle of freedom in the life of the individual believer and that of the community to which the believer belongs.

Bearing One Another's Burdens (vv. 1–3)

Verse 1 is extremely important in understanding the character of congregational discipline in the life of the early church. Paul returns to his favorite word of address for the Galatians: "brothers." When Paul does this, he not only indicates a new topic to be discussed, but he also reminds his readers of his affectionate regard for them.

The word for "caught" means literally to be "detected, overtaken, surprised."

Much speculation surrounds the exact meaning of Paul's comment, "if someone is caught in a sin."

What particular transgression Paul is referring to here, we do not know. Neither can we be sure whether Paul is referring to an actual "case study" that had come to his attention or if he is providing a general guideline for dealing with serious moral lapses among the Galatians.

Clearly, Paul is responding to a real-life situation in which concrete acts of wrongdoing, such as those he had just listed among the works of the flesh (5:19–21), are involved. Paul addressed his advice to those "who are spiritual," or the "spirituals." These are Christians who walk in the Spirit, are led by the Spirit, and keep in step with the Spirit.

It is best to understand the "spirituals" in the same kind of positive sense Paul uses it in 1 Cor. 2:15–3:4. There he contrasts the spiritual believers at Corinth with those who were "fleshly," or worldly minded. These were "baby" Christians more concerned with status and self-gratification than with the mind of Christ or service toward others.

Paul acknowledges that believers can and do sin and fall. While all sin is detestable before God and should be resisted, certain transgressors are especially hurtful to the fellowship of the church. These must be dealt with according to the canons of Christian discipline. Those who are spiritually minded and whose lives give evidence of the fruit of the Spirit have a responsibility to take the initiative in seeking restoration and reconciliation with those who have been caught in such an error.

How is this done? The lapsed brother or sister should be "restored gently." Here in Galatians Paul did not outline a specific procedure of church discipline, but he likely knew and presupposed the one given by Jesus in Matt. 18:15–17.

"Restore"

This word means "to put in order, to restore to its former condition." Elsewhere in the New Testament (Matt. 4:21; Mark 1:19), this same word is used for the mending or overhauling of fishing nets. It was also part of the medical vocabulary of ancient Greece, where it meant "to set a fractured or dislocated bone." In 1 Corinthians Paul uses this word in an ethical sense, exhorting the strife-torn Corinthian believers to put aside their dissensions so that they may be "restored" to unity in thought and purpose (1 Cor. 1:10).

Carrying One's Own Load (vv. 4–5)
Paul tells us bluntly, "Test yourself!" God will not hold us accountable for the gifts He gives others. The word for *test* is the word used for the fiery testing of gold in order to determine its purity. We are not to compare ourselves with "Pastor Jim," "Deacon Smith," or "Sister Jones." God wants us to bring our lives before the pages of His Holy Word.

There are two aspects of scrutiny and examination before God: (1) serious self-examination, and (2) evaluation that will be disclosed by

Christ when every believer appears before His judgment seat to give an account of the stewardship of his life. This verse has important implications for Christian spirituality, and we do well to heed its message.

During many parts of his letter to the Galatians, Paul presupposes a strong orientation to the doctrine of the last days. He places the verb for the carrying of one's own load in the future tense. This indicates that he was thinking not merely of an individual's bearing his own responsibility here in this life but more particularly the future reckoning of every Christian before the judgment seat of Christ.

Sharing with Teachers (v. 6)

Paul introduces another practical matter of behavior as an example of spiritual responsibility.

"Burdens and Loads"

Verses 2 and 5 seem to contradict each other. Thomas Lea points out that the two Greek words translated "burden" and "load" clarify the apparent difficulty. The term *burden* used in verse 2 describes a crushing weight or load in life. The term *load* (verse 5) was frequently used to refer to the pack of a soldier and described one of life's responsibilities which cannot be shared with another. Some burdens are so heavy, we need help with them. Others burdens we must carry ourselves.

Christians who are taught by a teacher are to contribute to that teacher's support. Paul may have feared that the mention of each person carrying his own load in verse 5 would lead the Galatians to abandon the support of those who ministered to him.

There seems to have been developing in the early church a group of teachers who gave enough time to this important task that they required some support from the congregation. Paul himself believed he had a right to support from those whom he served. He accepted help from the Philippians because they wanted to share in his ministry, but he refused support from the Corinthians because he was being accused of taking advantage of them (Phil. 4:14–18; 1 Cor. 9:6–18; 2 Cor. 11:7–11).

 What does verse 6 say to us today? First, the primary responsibility of pastors is to teach and preach the Word of God. All other aspects of the ministry, however worthy, must be subordinate to this fundamental task, for God has chosen "the foolishness of preaching to save them that believe" (1 Cor. 1:21, KJV).

Second, there is a special relationship between those who dispense instruction in the Word of God and those who hear and receive it. A workman is still worthy of his keep, and faithful pastors should not be taken for granted but rather recognized as a special gift from the Lord—one worthy of generous support. Finally, in receiving such support from their people, pastors should guard against two temptations.

1. Pastors who are richly blessed with material goods can forget the basic purpose of their ministry and become seduced by "the love of money [which] is the root of all evil (1 Tim. 6:10, KJV).

2. It is possible for a pastor to become so accustomed to a comfortable living that he functions as a mere hireling, forgetting that one day he must stand before Christ to give an account of the ministry to which he was called and the message he was privileged to preach.

Sowing and Reaping (vv. 7–8)

"Do not be deceived: God cannot be mocked. A man reaps what he sows" is a familiar and often-quoted verse. Its three statements are presented in staccato-like fashion.

Earlier Paul referred to the Galatians as "senseless" Christians who had been "bewitched" by some evil deceiver. Now he instructs them not to be misled in such a dangerous way. This is a strong statement that Paul uses twice in

"Mock"

This word is found nowhere else in the New Testament, although it is well attested in other Greek literature. It means literally, "turn up the nose in mockery or contempt." The Old Testament references are mostly to the mocking of God's prophets. Only once is this graphic word applied to a blasphemous mocking of God Himself.

"Corruption"

The word *corruption* conveys the idea of a corpse in the process of decomposition. The consequences of sins are nowhere more vividly seen than in the ravaging of the human body through disease, decay, and death.

1 Corinthians, in both cases as an introductory formula to a severe warning about immoral behavior.

Here in Galatians, the deception into which the Galatians were in danger of falling was even worse. Paul pleaded with them. God will not be mocked.

Paul moves on to apply these truths to the Galatian situation in terms of his earlier contrast of the flesh and Spirit.

If we continue to indulge in the works of the flesh, moving deeper and deeper into the pit of depravity, we can be certain of the harvest we will receive—corruption.

■ *A person who invests in the concerns of the flesh*
■ *reaps corruption. A person who invests in the*
■ *things of the Spirit reaps a harvest of eternal life.*

Don't Quit! (vv. 9–10)

Still using the agricultural imagery of planting time and harvest, Paul admonishes his readers to persevere in the faith, knowing that at the proper time God will fulfill His promise and bring to completion all things in accordance with the good pleasure of His own divine will.

Throughout Gal. 5–6 Paul instructs the Christians of Galatia to do a number of specific things: expel the agitators, love your neighbor as yourself, keep in step with the Spirit by manifesting the fruit of the Spirit in your lives, practice church discipline by restoring those who have fallen, bear one another's burdens, examine yourself in the light of the judgment seat of

Christ, and provide material support for those who instruct you in the faith. In verse 9 Paul summarizes all these duties under the rubric of "doing good."

■ *Paul's message to the Galatians is simply, "Don't*
■ *quit!" Faced with the temptation of legalism on*
■ *one hand and libertinism on the other, many of*
■ *Paul's converts in Galatia were beginning to lose*
■ *heart. Having begun well in the life of the Spirit,*
■ *they were in danger of losing their first*
■ *love—being diverted from witness and service*
■ *into petty bickering and greedy self-concern. To*
■ *these fatigued and spiritually exhausted Chris-*
■ *tians, Paul made his appeal: "Let us not become*
■ *weary in doing good."*

THE APOSTOLIC SEAL (6:11–16)

This verse begins the final paragraph of Paul's letter to the Galatians. In spite of its lack of personal greetings and intimate disclosures, Paul did not lose sight of his primary reason for writing his letter the Galatians.

Paul's Autograph (v. 11)

Most scholars and commentators believe that here Paul took the stylus from the hand of his secretary and finished the letter in his own handwriting, using unusually large letters to which he drew their attention.

Boasting in the Cross (vv. 12–16)

A Parting Blow (vv. 12–13). Throughout Galatians Paul waged a steady campaign against a group of false teachers, commonly known as Judaizers. These false teachers had sown great confusion among the apostle's recent converts

Why did Paul write in such large letters?

Much speculation revolves around this question. Was it Paul's poor eyesight (cf. 4:15) that required him to write in this unusual manner? Or was his writing hand twisted or defective as a result of some harsh persecution he had received? Was it that he was not a professional scribe but a workman more accustomed to shaping leather and making tents than using precise penmanship? All of these are intriguing possibilities, but none can be set forth with certainty.

It is likely that in addition to authenticating the letter as genuine and attesting that he had "meant what he said," Paul wanted to underscore and reemphasize both the central message of the letter and his own personal investment in its message.

by teaching that becoming Jewish was necessary for salvation. Paul's opponents evidently were Jewish Christian missionaries who were waging an aggressive evangelistic campaign of their own. It is not far-fetched to imagine that they had strong ties to the "mother church" at Jerusalem, especially to its ultra-legalistic wing.

In these two verses, Paul levels a dual charge against his opponents. He accuses them not only of dangerous doctrinal deviation but also of unscrupulous and unworthy motives.

Paul did not deny that there was an element of sincere and self-serving motivation among his opponents, but he did claim that there was a more sinister and self-serving motivation at work as well. These Judaizers wanted to boast and brag about how many Gentile Christians they had converted into Jewish proselytes.

The Cross and the New Creation (vv. 14–16.)
In contrast to the false teachers, who boasted about their accomplishments and who were especially proud of their success in winning Gentile believers to the requirement of circumcision, Paul declared in the strongest possible terms—"God forbid" (KJV)—that the only possible ground of his own boasting was the cross of the Lord Jesus Christ.

Paul developed the theme of boasting more than any other New Testament writer, for the kind of self-confident assertion it conveyed stood in marked contrast to the attitudes of humility called forth by divine grace. Thus, in Rom. 3:21–27, immediately following his exposition of the righteousness of God that is apart from the Law, Paul posed the question, "Where, then, is boasting?" His answer is dogmatic: "It is excluded!"

When confronted with the amazing grace of God, the very thought of self-glorification or spiritual ego-stroking vanishes.

Verse 16 is a conditional benediction: "Peace and mercy to all who follow this rule." This is no large-hearted conclusion like the one at the close of Paul's letter to the Philippians. Paul knew very well that he was writing to churches caught up in intense conflict over a serious doctrinal matter.

Rather than smoothing over the difficulty in the interest of a superficial harmony, Paul did the opposite: He emphasized the sharp differences between him and his opponents and forced the Galatians to make a choice. On one side of that choice was the apostolic curse; on the other, the apostolic blessing.

Brand Marks of Jesus (v. 17)

When Paul said that he carried around in his body the death of Jesus (cf. 2 Cor. 4:10), that he constantly bore the Lord's brand marks, he was referring to the actual scars of persecution and marks of physical suffering which he had received through his apostolic ministry because of his unflinching witness for the gospel.

Why did Paul mention the brand marks here at the very end of his letter?

1. Paul's readers would have identified the branding of the flesh with slavery.
2. Paul's reference to the brand marks also recalls his bitter opposition to the false teachers and their penchant for "boasting" in the flesh. Paul had already said that he would boast only in the cross of the Lord Jesus Christ (v. 14). With regard to Paul's ministry, the brand marks are a

Slaves in the ancient world frequently were marked with the insignia of their master as a badge of identification. Paul was saying, "Look, I too have been branded! I am a slave of my faithful Savior Jesus Christ."

seal and sure evidence of true doctrine and faith.

 3. The brand marks recall the fact of Christian baptism to which Paul refers in the heart of his letter (3:26–28). We cannot and should not try to duplicate Paul's sufferings, for they were unique to his own apostolic mission. But every believer who has been baptized "into the death of Christ" has become identified with Jesus in His sufferings no less than in the triumph of His resurrection. Baptism signals a separation from the world and a passage from the realm of Satan into the ownership of Christ.

■ *In this final paragraph of his letter, Paul*
■ *summarizes the main themes which he has*
■ *pursued throughout his letter. He did not lose*
■ *sight of his primary reason—to win the*
■ *Galatians back from the brink of apostasy to*
■ *a full-orbed faith in the one and only gospel*
■ *of Jesus Christ.*

BENEDICTION (6:18)

Paul had already provided a "benediction of peace" in verse 16. Here he concludes his letter with a second benediction. This one was a prayer for the grace of the Lord Jesus Christ to be with the Galatians, whom he again called his brothers. Paul began his letter with a customary salutation of grace (1:3), and he closed it with this same formula, pointing to the central theme that had been his primary concern throughout the epistle. This is a fitting conclusion to such a tumultuous letter. It is as though Paul is saying to the Galatians:

Dear brothers, in writing to you in this way I have put it all on the line. Now you know exactly the burden of my heart. I will end the letter as I began it, commending to you the awesome and marvelous grace of our Lord Jesus Christ. The only thing left for me to do is pray from my heart that Christ will confirm my labors among you, restoring you to the truth of the gospel and granting you the gift of perseverance unto life eternal. So may it be. Amen!

QUESTIONS TO GUIDE YOUR STUDY

1. Paul contrasted those who were "fleshly" with those who were "spiritual." What did Paul mean by "spiritual"?
2. What does it mean to "restore" a brother who has lapsed into sin?
3. Describe Paul's principle of reaping and sowing. How does he specifically apply it to the situation at Galatia?
4. What did Paul mean by boasting in the cross? How did he contrast his boasting to that of the false teachers?

REFERENCE SOURCES USED

The following list is a collection of the source works used for this volume. All are from Broadman & Holman's list of published reference resources. They will aid in your study, teaching, and presentation of the truths of Paul's epistle to the Galatians.

Cate, Robert L. *A History of the New Testament and Its Times.* An excellent and thorough survey of the birth and growth of the Christian faith in the first-century world.

Holman Bible Dictionary. An exhaustive, alphabetically arranged resource of Bible-related subjects. An excellent tool of definitions and other information on the people, places, things, and events of the Bible.

Holman Bible Handbook, 701–10. A comprehensive treatment of Galatians that offers outlines and commentary on key themes and sections. Provides an accent on the broader theological teachings of Galatians.

George, David. *Galatians* (Layman's Bible Book Commentary). A popular-level treatment of Paul's epistle to the Galatians. This easy-to-use volume provides a relevant and practical perspective for the reader.

George, Timothy. *Galatians* (The New American Commentary), vol. 30. A scholarly treatment of the text of Galatians that provides emphases on the text itself, background, and theological considerations.

Lea, Thomas D. *The New Testament: Its Background and Message,* 281–329. An excellent resource for background material—political, cultural, historical, and religious. Provides background information and broad overview of Galatians.

McQuay, Earl P. *Keys to Interpreting the Bible.* This work provides a fine introduction to the study of the Bible that is invaluable for home Bible studies, lay members of a local church, or students.

McQuay, Earl P. *Learning to Study the Bible.* This study guide presents a helpful procedure that employs the principles basic to effective and thorough Bible study. The various methods of Bible study are applied to the Book of Philippians. Excellent for home Bible studies, lay members of a local church, and students.

Robertson, A. T. *A Grammar of the Greek New Testament in the Light of Historical Research.* An exhaustive, scholarly work on the underlying language of the New Testament. Provides advanced insights into the grammatical, syntactical, and lexical aspects of the New Testament.

Robertson, A. T. *Word Pictures in the New Testament,* "The Epistles of Paul," vol. 4, 272–319. Insights into the language of the New Testament, Greek. Provides word studies as well as grammatical and background insights into Paul's epistle to the Galatians.